BFI Film Classics

W0230028

The BFI Film Classics series introduces, interprets and celebrates landmarks of world cinema. Each volume offers an argument for the film's 'classic' status, together with discussion of its production and reception history, its place within a genre or national cinema, an account of its technical and aesthetic importance, and in many cases, the author's personal response to the film.

For a full list of titles in the series, please visit
https://www.bloomsbury.com/uk/series/bfi-film-classics/

To my brother, a trailblazing film-maker in his own right

# Black Girl

## [La Noire de ...]

Vlad Dima

THE BRITISH FILM INSTITUTE
Bloomsbury Publishing Plc
50 Bedford Square, London, WC1B 3DP, UK
1385 Broadway, New York, NY 10018, USA
29 Earlsfort Terrace, Dublin 2, Ireland

BLOOMSBURY is a trademark of Bloomsbury Publishing Plc

First published in Great Britain 2025 by Bloomsbury on behalf of the
British Film Institute
21 Stephen Street, London W1T 1LN
www.bfi.org.uk

The BFI is a cultural charity, a National Lottery distributor, and the UK's lead organisation for film
and the moving image. We believe society needs stories. Film, television and the moving image
bring them to life, helping us to connect and understand each other better. We share the stories
of yesterday, search for the stories of today, and shape the stories of tomorrow.

A catalogue record for this book is available from the British Library.

Library of Congress Control Number: 2024949516

ISBN:    PB:    978-1-8390-2735-2
         ePDF:  978-1-8390-2737-6
         ePUB:  978-1-8390-2736-9

Produced for Bloomsbury Publishing Plc by Sophie Contento
Printed and bound in India

To find out more about our authors and books visit www.bloomsbury.com
and sign up for our newsletters.

# Contents

# Acknowledgments

I would first like to thank the editorial team at Bloomsbury/BFI for their steadfast support and professionalism. Secondly, I owe a great debt of gratitude to the anonymous readers, both at the proposal stage and at the manuscript stage. This book is much better thanks to their generous and thoughtful comments. Thirdly, many thanks to the staff at the Lilly Library at Indiana University, Bloomington, who helped me explore the Sembene archives and who then digitised three of the images used in this book. I am also grateful to Roger Hallas, my colleague and dear friend, who illuminated a particularly complex shot for me. A special thank you goes to Lauren Surovi, who patiently (and reassuringly) reads every word I write. Finally, even though he was not directly involved in this project, I must invoke Ken Harrow, now with the ancestors. My mentor from afar, then my friend and collaborator – you will forever be missed.

# Introduction

A young Black woman enters the frame from the right, her head turning to search for something seemingly elusive. She is inside a sparsely decorated apartment. Opposite her, on the left side of the frame, a wooden mask hangs prominently on the otherwise empty wall. In voiceover, the woman muses about her situation as she realises her predicament: she has become a de facto prisoner of the French family that hired her to be a nanny. This is Diouana, one of the most memorable characters in the oeuvre – both written and filmed – of Senegalese director Ousmane Sembene, and this is the scene that perfectly captures the drama and tensions of his groundbreaking *Black Girl*. This book is not only about her, of course, but it starts, builds around and ends with her story as it comes alive in this intimate moment of self-awareness. Diouana Gomis was a real-life person about whom Sembene once read an article in the newspaper *Nice-Matin*, which prompted him to write a short story and then adapt it to the big screen. Thus, the story of Diouana began well before the shooting of the film, and it continues to reverberate in the contemporary moment, if one considers, for example, its echoes in Nikyatu Jusu's horror *Nanny* (2022). Before addressing the contemporary period, though, let us begin with Ousmane Sembene, an inexorable fixture in the postcolonial African cultural milieu.

In the 1983 documentary *Caméra d'Afrique*, film-maker Férid Boughedir asks Sembene if Europeans understand his films. The venerable Senegalese director sardonically retorts, 'Europe is not my centre … The future does not depend on Europe.' He then refutes the idea that he might be a 'sunflower' that twists to follow the light of Europe. By way of conclusion, he confidently declares, 'I myself am the sun', thus placing himself not only at the centre of the world but at the centre of our universe. Similarly, in an interview with David

Ousmane Sembene

Murphy, he explains, 'I am African. [...] I don't have to search for an identity. I'm an African. For me, Africa is the centre of the world. The United States and Europe are on the periphery of my world' (2001: 228). While at first blush these declarations might come across as bombastic, even boastful,[1] it may be possible to think about Sembene in terms of a celestial body around which orbit numerous productions from francophone sub-Sahara and from the African diaspora. He is, without a doubt, one of the most important film-makers not just in the African cinescape, but in the history of cinema itself. Therefore, the starting point of this book aims to hypothesise Sembene as the centre of a particular version of African cinemas that has found lasting impact in World Cinema. What are the elements that revolve around him, both locally and internationally? This is one of the questions I seek to answer by exploring Sembene's 1966 film *La Noire de ...*/*Black Girl*, a *chef-d'œuvre* that finally made it into the 2022 *Sight and Sound* Greatest Films of All Time poll (released once every decade). This is a film around which one can map out Sembene's preceding literary output, his first film (a short titled *Borom Sarret* [1963]), and most films and books that would follow. In other words, *Black Girl* might be the nucleus to which one can attach Sembene's early career and whence one can anticipate most of the films that followed.

If *Black Girl* turned out to be the very spark that ignited the field of African cinemas, another relevant question follows: how far did this cultural map extend? Notably, the film found immediate success on the festival circuit, winning three awards the following year: the Jean Vigo prize at Cannes, the main award at the Festival mondial des arts nègres in Dakar and the Tanit d'or (the Journées cinématographiques de Carthage award) in Tunis. The local and international successes, combined with the memorable narrative, partially spurred on the fecund decade of the 1970s in African film-making. During this decade, the Senegalese Djibril Diop Mambety made the hallucinatory *Touki Bouki* (1973) and we witnessed the earnest beginning of the career of another Senegalese, Safi Faye,

with *Kaddu Beykat/Letter from My Village* (1976), to give but two
examples. As James Genova remarks, 'By the 1970s West Africa was
home to a burgeoning corps of innovative, dedicated, and active
film-makers who played a substantial role in elaborating an image-
Africa that challenged the prevailing tropes projected onto movie
screens around the world' (2013: 111). Among several worthy
names, Genova isolates Sembene as the 'dominant figure' whose
'work became iconic in articulating an African cinematographic
language and regime of representation that defined postcolonial West
African production for years to come' (ibid.). Sembene's evolution to
'dominant figure' owes a debt, by and large, to the impact of *Black
Girl*. The film reverberated across a wide swathe of African film-
making that followed it, having made a mark on the next generations
of African and African-diasporic film-makers (Abderrahmane
Sissako, Mahamat-Saleh Haroun, Alain Gomis, Jean-Pierre Bekolo,
Mati Diop, Maïmouna Doucouré and Nikyatu Jusu, among others).
To put this another way, and to mix metaphors, not only is Sembene
a guiding light, a sun, but his *Black Girl* casts a long shadow over
the subsequent productions of sub-Saharan francophone, French
francophone and even selective African American films.

Sembene adapted *La Noire de ...* from his own eponymous
short story, first published in the collection *Voltaïque* (1962,
translated as *Tribal Scars*, while the short story inexplicably becomes
'The Promised Land'). The film's original French title, *La Noire de ...*,
is far more intricate than the simplified English translation of *Black Girl*.
In French, the possessive '*de*' (of) clearly indicates that the character
belongs to something or to someone, while the ellipsis underlines the fact
that the possessor remains unknown. In both the short story and the
film, the plot centres on Diouana, a young woman from southern
Senegal (Casamance), who takes a job as a nanny working for a
white French family in Dakar. Following the family's invitation, she
then moves to the South of France (Antibes), where she faces months
of mistreatment and hard work, because the job turns out to entail
cleaning, grocery shopping and cooking, on top of taking care of

the children. Diouana becomes increasingly disillusioned with the realities of postcolonial France and with her precarious condition. In an act of both defiance and despair, she takes her own life.

The film version, shot in 35mm, in black and white, premiered on the African continent during the First World Festival of Black Arts in Dakar, April 1966. According to N. Frank Ukadike, '1966 was important for black African cinema' because it 'heralded the emergence of African fiction film' (1994: 77). The festival, a pet project of President Léopold Sédar Senghor, featured famous African and African American personalities, such as the Nigerian philosopher Wole Soyinka, American musician Duke Ellington, poet Langston Hughes and, of course, Senghor himself. In his early writings about African film-making, Paulin Vieyra mentions that the film was shown in Dakar months later, on 4 February 1967, during a gala at the Daniel Sorano Theatre. Following this event, Sembene took the film on the road, showing it in major Senegalese cities – Saint-Louis, Kaolack, Thiès and Ziguinchor – between February and March 1967 (Vieyra 1975: 165). In France, the film featured for two weeks in April 1967 at the recently opened Luxembourg cinema in the Latin Quarter of Paris (ibid.).[2]

### Biographical notes

To begin, a short note about the spelling of Sembene's name is warranted. I chose to omit the French grave accent (as in Sembène), because it appears to be the director's preferred spelling, according to David Murphy and Patrick Williams (2007: 50). Furthermore, using the accent highlights the overbearing cultural influence of France, against which the film-maker fought for most of his career.[3] In spite of these arguments, it may be worth signalling that the best-known biographer of Sembene, Samba Gadjigo, opts to use the grave accent. Naturally, wherever others have opted for the accented spelling, I have kept it in place.

While the date of his death, on 9 June 2007, is unassailable, Sembene's actual birthday remains uncertain. Officially, we have the date of 8 January 1923, which appears on several documents. However, Gadjigo does suggest that perhaps he was born a few days earlier, in December 1922, a claim that apparently comes from the film-maker himself (2010: 7–8). Paulin Vieyra explains that having a precise date for one's birth would be unusual in Africa at the time, and that one is born '*vers*' (around) a date; he completes his intervention by stating that Sembene was born on 1 January 1923, and that it took his parents 'eight days of reflection' to officialise his papers (2012: 9). Born in Ziguinchor, Casamance, in the southern part of Senegal, Sembene moved to the capital Dakar in 1938.[4] Soon after, he enlisted in the Sixth Colonial Infantry Regiment as a *tirailleur*, an experience that would later inspire him to make the tragically violent film *Camp de Thiaroye/The Camp*

Ousmane Sembene (seated, centre) on the set of *Xala* (courtesy Lilly Library, Indiana University, Bloomington, Indiana)

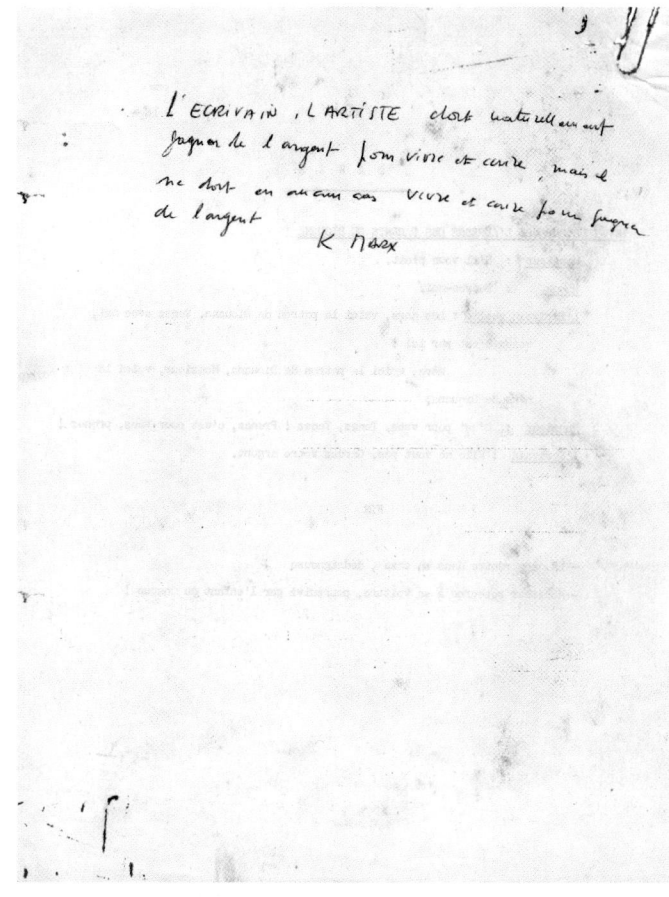

L'ECRIVAIN, L'ARTISTE doit naturellement
gagner de l'argent pour vivre et écrire, mais il
ne doit en aucun cas vivre et écrire pour gagner
de l'argent

K Marx

Sembene's handwritten note, quoting Karl Marx (courtesy Lilly Library, Indiana University, Bloomington, Indiana)

*at Thiaroye* (1988), and that coloured several other films and individual characters.[5] In fact, Sembene repeatedly used his own life as inspiration for his novels and films, and he was for the most part a 'largely self-educated man' (Murphy and Williams 2007: 50). After the war, he decided to go to France to pursue his interests in literature and writing. He arrived in Marseille, where he worked as a docker and discovered the ideology of the French Communist Party, Marxism, which began to shape him intellectually.[6] His experience in the South of France informed his first novel, *Le Docker noir/Black Docker* (1956). He followed this with *Oh pays, mon beau peuple!* (1957), which deals with the culture shock of returning to a home that no longer feels like home, especially when one comes back with a French wife. Sembene's next novel, *Les Bouts de bois de Dieu/ God's Bits of Wood* (1960), is often cited as his *chef-d'œuvre* and was loosely inspired by his short-lived experience working for the French West African railroad (but he did not participate in the historical strike of the railroad workers). In 1962, Sembene published the aforementioned collection of short stories, *Voltaïque*.

Countless interviews with Sembene have surfaced over the last few decades, but information about the film-maker was sparser at the outset of his career. Two of his interviews with Guy Hennebelle, from 1969 and 1971 respectively, provided the platform for several early references to his work, while Manthia Diawara's documentary *Sembène: The Making of African Cinema* (1994, co-produced with Ngũgĩ wa Thiong'o) gave Sembene ample space to describe his artistic thought process. In the 1969 interview, Sembene explains that he gravitated towards cinema and away from literature because of the high levels of illiteracy in Africa, which meant he 'could only touch a limited number of people' (Hennebelle 2008: 7). Speaking to a group of young people in the 1994 documentary, he also adds the following reason: 'To summarize history using our oral tradition, cinema is an important tool for us.' It is still to Hennebelle that Sembene explains how *Black Girl* was born and how he settled on the length:

I started to make this film without the authorization of the National Centre of the French Cinema. However, as it was a co-production between Domirev (Dakar) and *Les Actualités Françaises*, it needed one [...] Finally we realized that by presenting *La Noire de ...* as a short film (less than one hour) it would be easier to regularize the situation with the CNC. (ibid.: 9)[7]

The original intention was for the film to last ninety minutes, but the official Criterion version lists it at fifty-nine minutes. To get under the hour mark, Sembene claims to have 'cut all the colour scenes' (ibid.).[8] In the same interview, he shares the rationale for taking money from France (i.e. to help with finance and distribution), and states that the cost of making *Black Girl* was 'ten million [CFA]' (ibid.: 11).[9] In contrast, the budget for his next film, *Mandabi/The Money Order* (1968), the first film shot in an African language (Wolof), was 150 million CFA francs.[10] The high cost turned out to be a solid investment as *Mandabi* achieved one of Sembene's life goals: to move away from using French, because, as he often expressed, Africa could not be decolonised with foreign languages.[11] Using an indigenous language embodied Sembene's revolutionary attitude and material opposition to the remnants of the French colonial policy dubbed the Laval Decree, which until 1960 had prohibited Africans in France's colonies from making films or filming themselves. Such remnants could be observed in the capricious practices of financial patronage. For example, the French Ministry for Cooperation and Development refused 'to back Ousmane Sembene's *Black Girl/La Noire de …*, a bleak picture of French postcolonial attitudes, though the Ministry did subsequently buy the non-commercial distribution rights' (Armes 2006: 54–5). The well-documented financial struggles led Sembene to invent the expression '*mégotage*', a playful term for 'putting together [*bricolage*] a film on the cheap like a cigarette pieced together [*montage*] using butts [*mégot*]' (Harrow 2007: 238*n*5).

One of the often-quoted influences on Sembene's early cinematic career, Vittorio De Sica, was also known for cutting financial corners. Gadjigo mentions that Sembene frequently invoked De Sica's seminal neorealist film *Ladri di biciclette/Bicycle Thieves* (1948). Because he started his film-making career late, and during an incredibly important decade generally for film-making (with auteur cinema in full swing thanks to Ingmar Bergman in Sweden, Federico Fellini in Italy, the French New Wave in Paris and Akira Kurosawa in Japan, as well as the emergence of South American powerhouses Anselmo

Duarte and Glauber Rocha), Sembene has frequently been read by scholars against these movements and artistic efforts. His studying of film in the Soviet Union, between 1961 and 1962, further complicates the question of 'influence'. Yet, when asked directly in Diawara's documentary about images and films that first made an impression on him, Sembene irreverently claims he does not remember. In the end, I prefer to think of Sembene as creating art free of outside inspirations, and more tributary of his own written fiction. This premise allows for an unencumbered dive into the mechanics of his writing and film-making (i.e. detached from the aesthetic parameters of the Global North), which feed one another in a kind of closed circuit.

The main reason for this choice is that I question the sagacity of bridging Sembene's early career with Italian neorealism, Russian formalism or the French New Wave. While I drew similar parallels myself early in my academic career, such comparative models mostly help situate readers from the Global North, who may have prior knowledge of these artistic movements. Moreover, it runs the risk of subconsciously hierarchising Sembene and placing him below his European peers. So, although Gadjigo repeatedly talks about Sembene's love for De Sica, and Murphy and Williams describe the first period of his film-making career as 'highly influenced by Italian neo-realism', with films that 'explored the artistic possibilities and limitations of this style within an African context' (2007: 51), it would be preferable to think about Sembene outside such comparisons and categories, because these discussions could potentially perpetuate the erroneous narrative that (visual) culture from the Global North is superior to that of the Global South. Next, speaking of pitfalls, it may be instructive to revisit briefly the African artistic context in which Sembene made his first feature.

## African cinema(s)
It should be made clear from the beginning that it would be impossible to cover adequately the numerous debates about the definition of 'African cinema', or about its 'authenticity', in the short space allotted

to this book. As I have written elsewhere, the scholarship recognises that creating categories and labels that schematise 'African cinema' is no longer appropriate and has always been problematic. The currently acceptable nomenclature is to pluralise the term – African cinemas – which accounts for the wide cultural variety of film-making practices across the continent. That said, for the purposes of situating Sembene within the tradition of African film-making, it may be worth briefly revisiting the history of how we arrived at the current plural form of the original 'African cinema'.

African theorist and film-maker Paulin Vieyra identifies the 1924 short film *Ain-el-Ghezal* (or, *La Fille de Carthage/The Girl from Carthage*), by the Tunisian Samama Chikly, as the first recorded African film (1969: 41). A few years later, in *Le Cinéma africain des origines à 1973*, Vieyra declares that 'African film, born in 1924, reborn between 1953 and 1957, starts to develop after the independence of African nations' (1975: 19).[12] He emphasises that the continent would have to wait seventy-one years for a feature film made by an African – Sembene's *Black Girl* (ibid.: 162). Vieyra names himself, alongside Mamadou Sarr, and then separately, Blaise Senghor, Georges Caristan, Ababacar Samb Makharam and Momar Thiam, as rounding out this period of early cinematic efforts (ibid.: 374). Vieyra also points out that Senegal had no fewer than seventy cinema theatres in 1975, and that almost four and a half million spectators went to the movies in one year.[13] According to Roy Armes, Senegal accounted for 'about a fifth of francophone West African cinema in terms of both films and directors' (2006: 48), which echoes Vieyra's claim that Senegal was the most important African nation in terms of film production (1975: 155).

Vieyra, alongside theorists Teshome Gabriel and Manthia Diawara (who started writing about African film-making in the late 1980s and early 1990s, respectively), all favour the term 'African cinema'. Gabriel and Diawara were the first to define and provide a framework for this categorisation. They both came up with triads of categories[14] that correspond to Frantz Fanon's writings on decolonisation, leading to African film's transformation into an 'ideological tool' that deals with themes of resistance (Gabriel 1989: 31–5) and thus fitting within the parameters of the wider concept of Third Cinema.[15] Diawara introduced more and more nuance in his subsequent writings, and in 2010 he proposed an updated way to think about African film-making: instead of classic categories, he identified three more capacious and porous 'waves' (Arte, La Guilde des Cinéastes and New Popular African Cinema). In a response essay to Diawara's renewed attempt to define African cinema, Kenneth Harrow points out that a new 'Other' has emerged – African cinema itself – and any attempt to find an 'African specificity – in cultural, aesthetic, and cinematographic terms' means that one must 'go back to a past constructed largely around Sembène' (2015: 22). As a result, African film-making must be measured, discussed or dissected predominantly in relation to 'the Specter of Sembène' (ibid.: 26). Alexie Tcheuyap rhetorically wonders about the future of African film, too, and specifically about Sembene's 'lasting influence on African cinema' (2011b: 18). Sembene's ghost, much like Diouana's, still haunts the space of African cinema(s).

In his justification for pluralising African cinema, Tcheuyap first explains that Vieyra's argument for the use of the singular form was connected to the dominance of pan-Africanist thought. Second, since he is convinced that 'no single conceptualization is sufficient' when attempting to define African film-making (2011b: 24), Tcheuyap calls for the plural form '*African cinemas* in lieu of a monolithic and somehow misleading African cinema' (ibid.: 23). The plural form makes room not only for geographical and cultural diversity, but also for contemporary African film-makers who have experienced postcolonialism differently than the pioneers of the 1960s, and who have been more concerned with the negative effects of globalism and the neoliberal order. For example, Senegalese director Joseph Gaï Ramaka sees himself as 'a global human being and not in relation to a nation', who belongs to 'no cinema organization, or structure, African or non-African' (Tcheuyap 2011a: 19). Similarly, here's

Cameroonian director Jean-Pierre Bekolo's surprising, albeit purposely provocative, take: 'I don't know about African Cinema. I never studied it, and it's not my field' (Ukadike 2002: 220).

African cinemas have obviously changed since Sembene's debut. One of the key changes has to do with a slight shift from the overly pessimistic views on the postcolonial condition to a more positive outlook about the future. This trend, which the last part of this book discusses in more depth, partially came about thanks to the work of African public intellectuals, such as Achille Mbembe or Felwine Sarr. In *Sortir de la grande nuit/Out of the Dark Night* (2013), the philosopher Mbembe places Africa at the centre of the world and sees the continent as a catalyst for change,[16] whence a thought-world will begin to take shape, turning the continent into a cultural powerhouse. The economist and cultural writer Sarr envisions a bright future for Africa, too, given its youthful population and its vast resources, which were not fully depleted during colonialism. For him, Africa could still turn into the 'future Eldorado of global capitalism' (2016: 10). Both thinkers have continued to write about the need for radical changes in order to ensure a positive future: 'For the African continent, reopening the future begins with a reinvented relationship with its traditions and its cultural resources, avoiding the pitfalls of fetishization and self-hatred' (Sarr 2023: 120); and 'In order to settle their scores with their own history and give their imaginations urgently needed stimulation, Africans must purge themselves of the desire for Europe and learn to keep the best of themselves and their people in Africa' (Mbembe 2023: 93). Even though they likely did not have Sembene and Diouana in mind, Sarr and Mbembe's quotes could easily be entered into a discussion about *Black Girl*.

To end this introduction, it is important to acknowledge that my writing comes from a privileged position, as a white professor at an American institution that provides me with support that is not necessarily a given elsewhere. That said, I am a film theorist, a native Romanian who writes and teaches about film from Africa in both English and French, and I believe that my years working

in this field have made me keenly aware of the limits that come
with my positionality as an outsider and as a non-African person.
For more than a decade now, I have made a conscientious effort to
heed Mbembe's advice and to place Africa at the very centre of the
intellectual world. Hopefully, this has helped decolonise antiquated
ways of thinking, which have focused for far too long on the Global
North and its presumed primacy in terms of cultural production.
Along the way, I have come to think of my work as merely a building
block in the field of African cinemas, always in dialogue with the
work that preceded my own, while emphasising African voices and
shedding more light on the burgeoning presence of African culture in
the world.

# **1** Sonic Frames: Where It Begins

The structuring frame for this book begins and ends with a central episode from the film, namely Diouana's internal dialogue with a wooden mask that she has gifted to the French family. However, the initial focus of my analysis is on the voice – who speaks, what they say and why, and finally, where. In the final chapter, I return to the same scene but explore it in terms of the visual. Therefore, the focus of the book radiates outward (from this one moment to the rest of the film), then returns inward (back to the same moment following a wider exploration). The same dual movement occurs when considering the idea that African filmic culture operates by first moving outwards (from Sembene and *Black Girl* to other African and diasporic productions), then folding back upon itself (from the macro back to Sembene's long shadow).

As a sound studies scholar, I have long been interested in reversing the usual cinematic order of meaning (image + sound) to enquire what might happen if we first consider the impact of the sonic and secondarily, that of the visual.[17] Given its connection with orality, the field of African cinemas is a particularly auspicious domain for this kind of reversal.[18] Moreover, in the grand tradition of the *griot*, the West African oral performer and keeper of history after whom Sembene modelled his storytelling, the director believed it was imperative to use his voice, to *speak* truth to power and to instil the idea of resistance in his countrymen.

Speaking of voice, the role of Diouana is technically played by two actors: Senegalese actress Mbissine Thérèse Diop plays the visual part, while Caribbean singer/actress Toto Bissainthe speaks her words. It is worth noting that the voices for the two main white actors, Monsieur and Madame, are also provided by two different actors. It should also be specified that the choice of adding voices and sound in postproduction had little to do with a particular directorial vision, and everything to do with financial limitations (direct sound and recording being prohibitively expensive).[19] Regardless, the dual part turns into a happy accident of history, as the splitting of Diouana's voice and body across two actors further complicates her identity in interesting ways. In other words, the fact that a character whose identity eludes her – mostly because she is denied a choice – is played by two women underlines the physical and emotional fragmentation we witness on the screen.

Olivier Barlet refers to Bissainthe's voice as giving the visual actress on screen more volume, and he calls it 'a voice of desire, of doubt, and of *flesh*' (1996: 182, my emphasis).[20] It is the last descriptor that interests me the most, because it makes the voice material. The voice is a complicated part of our bodies, and, as a matter of fact, the very word 'part' is the reason why it is so complex – is it really a part of our bodies? The sound of the voice escapes our bodies, never to return, and it is simultaneously non-material (i.e. air vibration) and material as it extends our physical bodies, projecting them into whatever direction the voice speaks. Indeed, I think of the voice as an extension of our bodies that, momentarily at least, widens the physical space we occupy in the world. In other words, it is not the body (or the throat) that carries the voice, but rather it is the voice the propels the body through space, our bodies constantly trying to keep up or catch up with the words that escape through our mouths.[21] The way I conceptualise sound as voice (or, noise as voice, since only an 'elusive and uncertain' line separates the two; Dolar 2006: 13) finds an apt manifestation in Sembene's Diouana. Because her voice is dubbed in postproduction by another actress, there is a sense of mismatch throughout the film.[22] The proficiency of Bissainthe's accented but melodious French does not quite match the information from the narrative that Diouana cannot read or write in French. This generates a spurious aural fullness, because the voice is sufficiently in command of the French language (minus the francophone accent). So, the voice separates itself from Diouana and

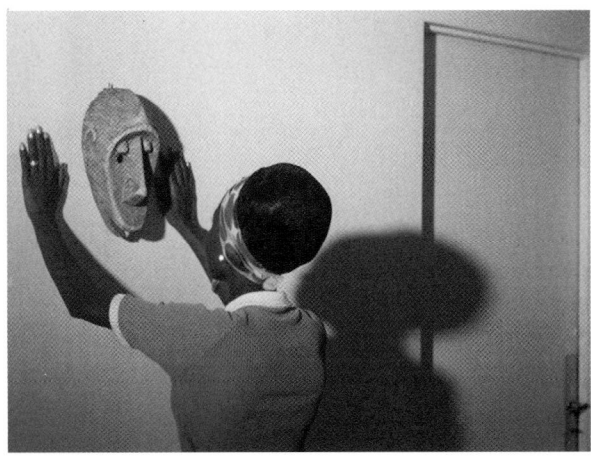

becomes more of a narrative vehicle to get the story across. Finally, Bissainthe's Haitian origins adds another dimension to the character, as it stretches the sonic pan-African body of Diouana from Dakar to the Caribbean, by way of France.

The analysis begins *in medias res*: Diouana stands in the living room, facing the mask on the wall, while two shadows take shape on either side of it. As she shares her thoughts in voiceover, she physically moves off screen. For a moment, all that is left in the shot are the mask and the character's lingering shadow(s). The body literally disappears, but the voice remains unaffected by this material change, and goes on uninhibited, still aurally full, propelling the physical body forward. The voice transforms into a sonic object, adorning the walls of the soundtrack, much like the literal mask on the wall. In fact, a sonic transfer occurs, as the voiceover travels from the visual body to the object on the wall that momentarily speaks to us. There is a further dialogue at play here, between the not-so-silent mask and Diouana's voice, which is matched by the visuals.

A disembodied voice such as Diouana's (I contend that it remains 'disembodied' throughout, because the voice and the body do not match) should garner Michel Chion's powers of the acousmatic:

ubiquity, panopticism, omniscience and omnipotence (1999: 23–4). However, as the voice remains enveloped in the restrictive space of the apartment, such powers are muted. Therefore, sound as voice textually suggests that Diouana might be a living-dead figure: 'voice is neither dead nor alive: its primordial phenomenological status is rather that of the living dead, of a spectral apparition that somehow survives its own death, that is, the eclipse of meaning' (Žižek 1996: 103). Diouana's meandering voice also recalls the process of de-acousmatisation, which refers to a moment in film when a previously unknown source for a sound or voice is visually revealed. Here, Mladen Dolar points out a potential problem:

The acousmatic voice is simply a voice whose source one cannot see [...] but even when it finds its body, it turns out that this doesn't quite work, the voice doesn't stick to the body, it is an excrescence which doesn't match the body.

(2006: 60–1)

Žižek proposes that the body is indeed hollowed out by its own voice:

The voice acquires a spectral autonomy, it never quite belongs to the body we see, so that even when we see a living person talking, there is always some degree of ventriloquism at work: it is as if the speaker's own voice hollows him out and in a sense speaks 'by itself,' through him. (1996: 92)

Diouana's voice, which does not even belong to the visible body, represents a classic case of ventriloquism. Sembene interferes at this moment, too, as the screenplay puts words in her mouth. It is worth repeating that the screenplay was adapted from a short story, also written by Sembene. The point is that Diouana's voice carries with it a significant trace of Sembene's creative voice because there are two overlapping levels of written words – story and script – that generate the actor's spoken lines. The result is that even what appears to be aural fullness, by way of the voiceover, is just an empty sonic shell carrying Diouana's visible body through the motions.

As the character moves to the left of the frame, the next shot pans left inside the living room, revealing the rest of the wall, which is empty. The voiceover narration supports the projected emptiness: 'Where are the people who live in this country?' Then the next shot takes emptiness to an extreme by revealing the window overlooking the blackness of the night. The camera continues to pan left as if trying to find proof of life in the darkness, while Diouana asks herself another rhetorical question: 'Is this France?' To summarise, Diouana's visual body first appears, then disappears, and when it re-emerges after this scene, it does so as a fragmented body, cinematically speaking. The voiceover, though, remains steady and material, the veritable 'flesh' to which Barlet alludes. Furthermore, it leaves a sonic shadow that lingers throughout the film, as the visual body attempts to catch up with her inner thoughts. In short, the sonic body is narratively more impactful, but it still voids the character of any significant powers.[23]

One potential power that the voiceover does have is that it gives the character access to places and moments from the past. There are two flashbacks in the film, during which the audience pieces together Diouana's backstory: the moment she was hired by Madame in Dakar, her relationship with a young man and the invitation to come to Antibes. As she complains about the fact that back home she only took care of the children and did not have to do chores, the voiceover clearly belongs to Diouana in Antibes, or present-day Diouana. However, what the visual reveals is past Diouana accompanying the three children in the streets of Dakar. This set-up further underlines the split between sonic body and visual body, as they are temporally separated, too. As such, the body of the character is completed via a temporal game of moving to the past visually, while remaining entrenched in the present through the voice. The second time Diouana travels back in time to Dakar in her memories, she also accesses them via voiceover. In other words, her voice allows her to move back and forth in time, though this might have less to do with 'power'. Instead, it may be a palliative measure, as she retrieves her memories in order to look forward to the future. The only reason she 'fails' to arrive at that future is because her isolation and the spectre of colonialism slowly erode all hope.

The voiceover dominates the soundscape of the scenes in the past, too, while accompanied by empathetic music (i.e. matching the introspective mood of the moment), coming from the gently plucked strings of a xalam. This is the same instrument we hear extensively in Sembene's *Borom Sarret*,[24] in which the director contrasts the sounds of the xalam with European music: the passage from traditional Senegalese tones to classical music overlaps with the visual transition from a shanty town to the affluent (and white) 'Plateau'. Sembene returns to a similar musical contrast in *Black Girl*: when Diouana arrives in Marseille and then immediately post-death, very cheerful piano hall music plays on the soundtrack, as opposed to the more traditionally African sounds that accompany the flashbacks in Dakar.[25]

Like the dejected cart driver, Diouana begins to wonder what the people from back home would think of her. She imagines them seeing her happy and leading a great life. Then she immediately corrects the record: 'For me, France is the kitchen, the living room, the bathroom and my bedroom.' Standing in front of a closed window, Diouana delivers one of the most impactful lines of the film: 'Is this black hole France?' There are a lot of layers of meaning that emerge from this line. At a basic level, Diouana contrasts her expectations and vivid fantasies about France with the literal darkness outside the window. That darkness is not only literal, though; it is very much figurative, as well. France is a black hole – it sucks the life out of Diouana. From the closed window, Diouana walks away, and in the next shot she is in her room undressing to get into bed. She asks herself, 'What am I here?', in a clear signal that phrasing the question with the interrogative pronoun 'who' no longer makes sense. She goes through the various possibilities (the cook, the cleaning woman, the washerwoman), and then states that she is alone. She enumerates the clothing items that Madame had given her in Dakar, 'her old dresses, her old slips, her old shoes', and as she shares this new list, we watch her undress in a long take that drastically slows down the pace of the narrative. Finally, she asks one more rhetorical question, 'Is this living in France?', which is followed by a fade-out, a cinematic black hole that literally ends the scene, her day and her thoughts in darkness.

The last moments in Diouana's life are suffused in a metaphorical darkness that the character also recounts in voiceover. Following a fight with Madame over the ownership of the mask, Diouana packs her bag while telling herself that 'never again will the mistress scold me'. A series of various actions and tasks that Madame required her to do follows (make coffee, make rice, take off your shoes, wash this shirt, etc.), and Diouana punctuates each of these with the declaration 'never again'. She continues to stress these words, which culminate in the proleptic completion of the phrase, 'Never again Diouana.'[26] Having packed, she places the mask on top of the suitcase, then walks away towards the bathroom, still telling herself *jamais plus* and that Madame would never lie to her again. As she approaches the bathroom door, Sembene goes into a point-of-view (POV) shot that reveals the nothingness lying in front of Diouana's eyes. The shot is blurry and basically fades into the white of the bathroom door. When the door opens wide, it reveals another layer of whiteness (that of the bathroom wall). Sembene stays on the empty wall and opts for a dissolve that

takes the audience to the same wall, but with Diouana's house dress
hanging off it. The next cut reveals a gruesome image: Diouana in the
blood-spattered bathtub, a bloody razor falling from her right hand.
The razor appears in close-up in the next shot, covered in blood, along
with blood drips on the carpet and on the side of the tub. A third shot,
from a slightly higher angle, shows Diouana's entire body from head
to toe. Water still drips from the tap and the concentric ripples give
off the sense of movement, which Diouana's body lacks. In death, the
body has finally caught up with the voice.

## The short story

There are several echoes of the short story in the film. The literary
version tells the familiar story of the young émigrée, Diouana. One
particularly significant difference in the original plot is that Sembene
reveals the suicide on the first page of the short story, while in the
film he chooses to place it towards its conclusion. The decision to
start with Diouana's death turns the short story into a quasi-mystery
(i.e. why did she kill herself?). The task for the reader is to fill in the
blanks as we work our way backwards through the narrative. While
the written story fulfils this narrative intent, the cinematic effect of

seeing Diouana in the bathtub, naked and bloodied, represents a much more intense emotional payoff, to my mind.

Another noteworthy difference between the short story and the film is that in the former, it is emphasised that Diouana suffers from depression and homesickness. The mention of the latter is barely visible in the body of the article that Sembene briefly shows at the end of the film. Moreover, since it is untranslated, the reference to homesickness is only accessible to French speakers who can identify the word '*cafard*' (fit of depression) at the bottom of the screen. The title of the intradiegetic article simply describes the act of suicide and does not offer a reason. However, in the short story Sembene transcribes from the article the following sentence: 'At Antibes, a homesick [*nostalgique*] Black woman cuts her own throat' (1987: 99). Diouana misses her home, that's undeniable, but she is also dealing with loss – separated from family, from her country and from her idealised version of France, which does not align with reality. This series of losses might transform nostalgia into something more akin to mourning or melancholia, but that would take us too far off the current road, as it were. A more immediate question that arises relates to the graphic reveal of the manner of suicide: Could someone really

**ES FAITS DIVE**

| l de linge et de un cultivateur t-Pancrace | A ANTIBES **Une jeune négresse se tranche la gorge dans la salle de bains de ses patrons** | Le pend dans les a été |
| --- | --- | --- |
| **ier-peintre arrêté eté de Nice** | | ... mais on les causes |
| ier, M. Joseph Pas- ur, demeurant à -Joséphe », chemin quartier Saint-Pan- u commissariat du qu'un vol de linge pour une valeur avait été commis | Gomis Diouana, une jeune né- gresse de Dakar, a mis fin à ses jours dimanche, vers 13 h., en se tranchant la gorge dans la salle de bains de sa patronne. Lorsque des coloniaux rentrant en France s'étaient attachés les services de la jeune Gomis Diouana, qui avait vu le jour à Boutoupa, au Sénégal, ils n'avaient certes pas pensé que leur bonne aurait le mal du pays au point de se trancher la gorge un jour de cafard. Parlant | Hier matin, n cabre découvert jeunes gens se bois situés derr des Terriers en tibes, bois d'un et où le hasar découvrir dimar le cadavre d'un pendu à une chêne. Le commissai bes, en raison |

cut across their entire neck? Thus, the short story briefly turns into a whodunnit because it throws into question whether or not she was murdered, and in fact, the inspector literally poses the question 'Why do you think it was suicide?' (ibid.: 86) at the outset.

The beginning of the short story also evidences Sembene's cinematic writing style. The omniscient narrator (who, by definition, takes away all the narrative power from Diouana) begins on the Riviera, then moves to the street, followed by the villa, and eventually settles inside the space of the house. The progression from wide to specific is akin to that of situating a spectator in cinematic space by slowly decreasing distance, starting with an establishing shot, and progressing by way of multiple cuts all the way into a close-up. The omniscient narrator not only drowns out the voice of the main character, but he also allows himself to even pass judgement on the gullible maid (for example, he calls her voice 'childish'; ibid.: 88). The disparaging undertone of the short story may prevent the readers from developing as strong an identification with the character as they do in the film.

Another critical change is that in the short story, there is no boyfriend. Instead, Sembene includes a character named Tive Correa, who has lived in France for twenty years. In spite of the fact that he is a meandering drunk, Tive represents the voice of reason that warns Diouana of the pitfalls of migration. Diouana does not listen to him, just as she does not let herself be influenced by the young man, or fiancé, in the film. Finally, the short story features at its conclusion a poem. David Murphy is one of the few scholars who discusses the companion poem at length (2001: 50), and according to his analysis, Diouana 'is now the mother of all Africans' (ibid.), which makes the character exceed the confines of the short story and film.[27] Sembene's well-known moniker of 'father of African film' intimates that he, too, transcends limitations. We can safely hypothesise that Sembene's unforgettable cultural legacy began not with one but two interlocked entities – he, as the father, *and* Diouana, as the mother of African cinemas.

## **2** Characters

The second chapter examines in more detail the film's characters and their motivations, but it begins with Diouana's mental and physical connection with Dakar, by way of her literary link with the island of Gorée. In developing *Black Girl*, Sembene took inspiration from a news item in the daily *Nice-Matin* about Diouana Gomis's suicide in 1958. Scholar Doyle Calhoun tracked down Diouana's actual case file in Nice, and published the results of his research under the provocative title 'Sembène's "Black Girl" Is a Ghost Story' (2021). Calhoun also unearthed her death warrant in Antibes, the official report of the suicide of a 31-year-old in the Nice regional archives (stating the 'likely cause of death: suicide'), as well as the newspaper that appears at the end of the film: 'This is no ordinary prop. Sembène is winking at us – nodding to the genesis of his film in a very material way' (ibid.). With the help of these items, Calhoun carefully reconstructs the story of the real Diouana, who died in her employers' bathroom on 22 June 1958, after only three months in France. Like the fictional version, the real Diouana came from Ziguinchor, specifically from a small village called Boutoupa.[28] The fact of her real existence adds another fascinating layer to the multitude of versions (literary, sonic, visual) and the 'shadows' that ensue. The spectral shadow of the real Diouana (a ghost, as Calhoun rightfully indicates) hovers over the short story, while the saturnine literary ghost of Diouana enters the film via the voiceover,[29] and the visual body of Diouana spawns its own shadows.

In the short story, Sembene connects her with another shadow, that of the island of Gorée, which puts Diouana in dialogue with other ghosts: the dead of the transatlantic slave trade. The literary Diouana, still in Dakar, looks out of the window and suddenly loses herself in thought ('*transportée*', in the original French), mesmerised by the sight of birds flying in the sky. Sembene brilliantly connects the figurative meaning of the word '*transportée*' (lost) with its literal meaning ('transported') and adds the subtle image of Gorée Island, barely visible at the horizon (1987: 90). There are other instances in the film when Diouana gets lost in thought, such as on her arrival in Antibes or as she contemplates images from around Dakar during the flashbacks, but the link with Gorée carries more significance.

The island, sitting just west of Dakar, was (along with Saint-Louis) among the first official French settlements in Senegal. The French took the island from its initial colonialist settlers, the Portuguese, and while it changed hands several times during the colonial period, the island remained a hub of the transatlantic slave trade. Currently, it hosts a museum dedicated to this colonialist past. Clint Smith's book *How the Word Is Passed: A Reckoning with the History of Slavery Across America* (2021) dedicates an entire chapter to visiting Gorée and its museum, the House of Slaves (Maison des Esclaves). Smith disputes the high number of slaves reported to have passed through Gorée and offers a lower estimate of about '33,000 enslaved people' (ibid.: 251). Eloi Coly, the Senegalese curator, pushes right back:

the slave house crystallizes all of the slave trade [...] It's a *symbol* of the slave trade [...] The number of slaves is not important when you talk about memory [...] When we talk about memory, we have to stand in the principles. One slave is too much. (ibid.: 252)

Regardless of the actual numbers, Gorée Island remains one of the archetypal symbols of slavery in Senegal and it often appears in Senegalese cinema.

The island turns into a spectral presence, a shadow of the colonial era, in multiple films by Djibril Diop Mambety but most prominently in *Touki Bouki* and *Hyènes/Hyenas* (1992). Joseph Gaï Ramaka shot the beginning of *Karmen Geï* (2001) on the actual island. Sembene invokes Gorée elsewhere, too. In *Faat Kiné* (2001), the island is a marker of distance, as the titular character complains to her daughter, who wants to study in Canada, that she never went 'beyond Gorée'. There is a hidden meaning in Faat's choice, suggesting that she has not got 'past' Gorée and its associated trauma. Diouana finds herself mentally transported away, having literally taken a boat to arrive in France, and like the victims of colonialism, she also becomes a slave at the end of the journey. Finally, the meaningful connection between Diouana and the island can easily extend to include Bissainthe, who is from Haiti – one of the destinations of the slave trade that originated on the western coast of Africa.

## Madame

Perhaps the simplest way to read Madame is to assign to her the role of the 'bad guy'. Her upscale, buttoned-up outfits (highlighted by the impenetrable sunglasses) and her supercilious attitude indicate her social status and impart an air of superiority. At first glance, her character seems to lack nuance – she is affluent, entitled, white. She incessantly chastises Diouana for wearing her chic dress while working, although the dress was a gift from Madame herself. Madame even rings a little hand bell to get the maid's attention and

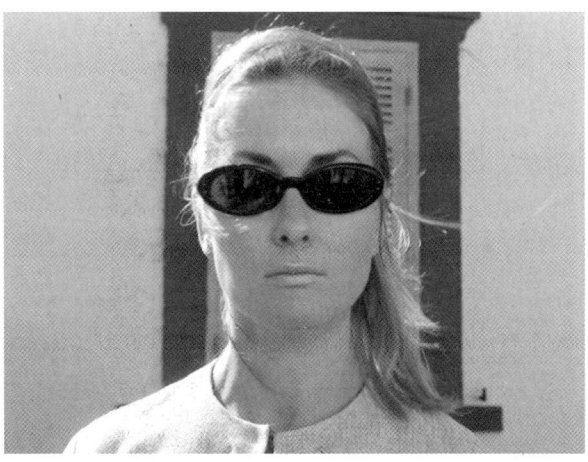

allows others to partake in the abuse. During the dinner the couple
organises at home for other white friends, the group discusses the
situation in Senegal off screen, while Diouana is in the kitchen. They
mention President Senghor, suggesting that the country will remain
stable as long as he stays in power. The fact that the French white
characters speak positively about Senghor's government is Sembene's
way of criticising it (i.e. this may be a government more aligned
with French sensibilities than protecting Senegalese interests). After
Diouana serves the coffee, one of the female guests asks, 'Does she
speak French?', which brings to mind Senghor's most controversial
decision, to preserve French as the main language of the Senegalese
educational system. Madame responds that Diouana does not, to
which the guest's husband quips that 'she understands', as his wife
completes his thought by adding, 'instinctively'. Just in case the
racism does not register with the audience, Madame goes on 'like an
animal'. Ironically, in the short story, Madame cannot pronounce her
name (Sembene 1987: 98), which vexes Diouana and underlines the
hypocrisy of questioning her language skills.

If there is more nuance to the character of Madame, it would
involve her marital situation with Monsieur, as she often appears
exasperated with him. In her estimation, he does not take enough
action, does not do enough to help her berate Diouana and probably
has a drinking problem. However, the two white characters do
not require full development and, for the grander purposes of the
narrative (which presents them as aggressors), they must be less
contoured. In other words, they need to remain as caricatures, so as
not to humanise them to a degree where they become sympathetic.
Thus, Madame stays one-dimensional – the evil coloniser who abuses,
who promises one thing and delivers another, who gives gifts but does
not want Diouana to wear them as she so desires. Her toxic behaviour
and churlish demands align perfectly with colonial attitudes.

In a moment that directly points to Madame's aggression, she
goes to Diouana's room and hits her violently across her middle
to wake her up. When Madame walks back into the living room,

she notices the disappearance of the mask from the wall. Ignoring Monsieur, who says they should let Diouana be, Madame goes back to the bedroom, where she notices the mask on the floor and picks it up (at this point, Diouana is also on the floor, having collapsed following the belated receipt of her salary from Monsieur). Madame's re-entry makes Diouana jump out of her stupor. She springs to her feet, grabs the other side of the mask and exclaims, 'It's mine!' Sembene moves the camera up, tracking the fight over the mask in a high-angle shot. The women go in circles, then Sembene shifts to alternating POV shots as the tussle continues. When Monsieur enters the room, Madame explains that Diouana has taken the mask. His surprisingly logical response that the mask belongs to Diouana ('She gave it to you!') leaves Madame unsatisfied. The fight ends, and Monsieur and Madame exit the room quietly.

## Monsieur

While Madame is the more visible tormentor, Monsieur plays a more subtly menacing part. One noteworthy moment that has not garnered enough attention in the scholarship on *Black Girl* is the suspicious cutaway shot from Diouana hiding in the bathroom to a sleeping Monsieur in the bedroom, with a nude magazine lying open beside him. Just moments before, during the dinner sequence, one of the male guests had made a ribald comment, 'I hope it's an aphrodisiac', referring to Diouana's *mafé* sauce. This exclamation comes from off screen, as Diouana refills a plate with rice in the kitchen, so the words sonically overlap the visual presence of the character. Moreover, we could safely assume that it is the same guest who stands up and kisses her on both cheeks, while sharing that he has never kissed a 'Black woman'. Although he does ask for permission, he does not wait for her verbal consent, and when he kisses her cheeks, Diouana's body appears insensate. This outrageous harassment of Diouana does not visibly extend to Monsieur. However, the proximity of the two moments and the connection forged via the montage cannot be ignored, indicating there might just be something else lurking beneath the surface.

The hidden relationship between Monsieur and Diouana in the film version could be a remnant of the whodunnit aspect from the short story. There is another mystery here, and the short story does include a comment about the cook, Samba, who 'suspects' that something is afoot between Monsieur and Diouana (Sembene 1987: 91).

Monsieur's more obvious transgression is that he loves to drink.[30] During the cringe-worthy scene when Diouana serves her rice to the guests, Sembene cuts to Monsieur, who pours himself a glass of wine, which he proceeds to gulp down swiftly. In a later scene, Diouana enters the apartment having returned with groceries, and Madame interrogates her husband about why Diouana appears to be wasting away. True to his usual taciturn self, Monsieur offers a half-hearted comment about the climate not agreeing with her, then pours himself some whisky, labelled *Black & White*, to which he adds water. Sitting across from him, Madame's legs are visible, resting on the coffee table. In the background we can see Diouana, framed by a multitude of straight lines – the door to the kitchen, the window above her head, the refrigerator behind her – all of which contribute to the sense that space is narrowing around her. I will return to Sembene's penchant for intradiegetic frames in the last chapter.

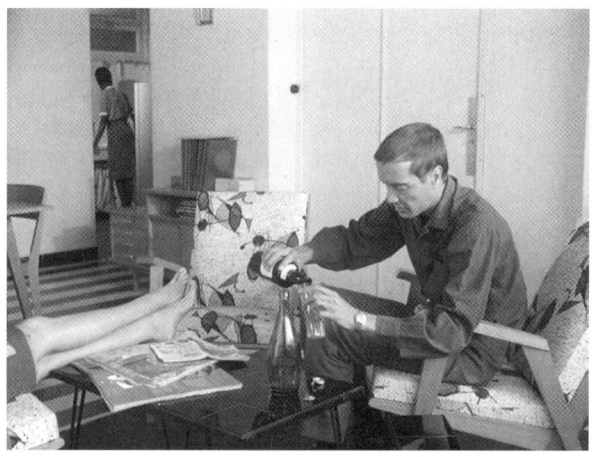

However, it is important to underscore here that Diouana is caught between the two white bodies, forming a triangle. Moreover, Sembene employs deep focus, which makes Diouana visible and simultaneously present with the two white bodies in the foreground, while keeping her at a cinematic distance.

Having mixed his drink, Monsieur picks up the glass and walks away. As he tells his wife that he is going to take a nap, the camera pans left to follow him, and the triangle dynamic shifts, placing him in between the two women. In this frame, Madame's body is almost entirely visible in the foreground of the shot. Her aggressive response, 'Yes, you'd better', indicates that she thinks he has had too much to drink and needs to sleep it off. He does not respond, which is often the choice he makes when interacting with her. On his way to the bedroom, he stops in the kitchen doorway and looks at Diouana, who has her back to him. It is difficult to interpret the meaning behind this look, but Diouana does turn around, sensing his presence. She looks him up and down, as she continues to dry a glass. Monsieur looks back at Madame and then again at Diouana, completing the same triangle as above, but without the need for any cutaway shots. Madame remains off screen, but he seems to be caught between the

two women. His 'predicament' is far less clear than Diouana's – is he thinking about saying something to Diouana to appease his wife, or is he considering something else entirely?

Next, Sembene returns to the previous angle, with Madame in the foreground lighting up a cigarette, and Diouana in the far background, still in the kitchen. Following another quick shot in the

kitchen while she cleans, Diouana looks back towards the couple's bedroom. The next shot transitions to Monsieur, sleeping peacefully. There is an empty glass on the nightstand, a *BRIK* comic book on his chest, along with the opened nude magazine lying suggestively by his right arm. Paulin Vieyra considers that Monsieur's reliance on comics and alcohol to get through the day is indicative of '*la démission de l'homme*' (the demise of the man), which, according to him, is more and more common in western civilisation (1975: 164). Generalisations aside, Vieyra glosses over the nude magazine, which could point to solitary sexual activity by Monsieur, or to more pernicious intentions towards Diouana. After Madame leaves the apartment to take a walk, Diouana comes into the living room to clean up the coffee table. At this juncture, Sembene inserts a second shot of Monsieur sleeping, slightly changing the previous angle to show that one of his legs dangles off the bed – he has passed out. The lamp illuminates only half of his face, underlining the character's ambiguous status, while the rest of his body lies in obscurity – perhaps he is a monster lying in the dark. In a later scene, as Diouana laments her condition, Sembene similarly lights up just half of her face, but the meanings of these shadows vary considerably

between Monsieur (hiding something or hiding himself) and Diouana (expressing anguish). Nevertheless, the double return to Monsieur leads us to understand that Sembene really wants to emphasise that there is more to him than meets the eye.

Among all his faults, visible or suggested, Monsieur may have one redeeming quality: he appears to care about his children, or at the very least, his eldest son, with whom we see him interact a couple of times. At the breakfast table, he checks on his son's well-being, and when they return from shopping to find Diouana out of commission, he carries Philippe from the armchair, where he has fallen asleep, to the bed. The fatherly behaviour extends on occasion to Diouana, but it is nuanced by a colonialist tinge. Nowhere is this clearer than in the scene when Monsieur reads Diouana a letter from her mother.

After he summons Diouana from the kitchen, he asks her if he should read it. She agrees, and the three characters sit around the living-room table. Monsieur tells the maid that the letter is from her mother and proceeds to read it out loud. In the letter, the mother complains that she has had no news since her daughter's departure, that her health is deteriorating, and she asks Diouana why she has not sent any money home. It also includes an accusation that

Diouana 'squanders' her wages and a reminder that Madame is a
'great lady', who gave her gifts and agreed to reply to her letters,
since Diouana cannot read or write. Indeed, Monsieur offers right
away to scribe a response, which he commences and then asks
for input from Diouana. When met with silence, he proceeds and,
speaking to himself as he writes, puts down that Diouana is in good
health. At this point, Diouana takes her mother's letter and tears it
up. In voiceover, she declares, 'That's not true. And it's not my letter.
My mother didn't write it.' As horrible as Monsieur and Madame
are, it is quite possible that Diouana refuses to accept the reality of
this letter. Had we not met the public letter writer back in Dakar,
perhaps an argument to support her claim could be made. However,
the letter does sound legitimate. To remind us of an earlier moment,
when Diouana reflects about what people back home might think
of her, she imagines them (her mother included) supposing that she
is living the high life. Diouana walks away in tears, frustrated that
she cannot write back herself to tell her mother the truth about
Madame's 'kindness'. She shares in voiceover that she is a prisoner,
and moments later specifies, 'I am their prisoner. I don't know anyone
here. No one in my family is here. That's why I'm their slave.'

Monsieur is the one who controls the family's finances, and in a sense, he is the one who finally reduces Diouana to a desperate state. He walks into her room, asks her if she is sick and then if she wants her money. He takes out a wad of cash and offers her twenty thousand francs, then specifies ten thousand CFA francs. As he hands Diouana the banknotes, she drops the first one, then begins to crumble as if under the weight of the world. The few notes that drop to the floor, which are also visible when Diouana returns the money to him, are ten-franc banknotes featuring Voltaire, which indicates that he did not have the full amount owed to her. Diouana falls to the floor in the foetal position, the camera following her, and shooting her from a high angle, but not from Monsieur's POV (i.e. that of the colonial/postcolonial father). It is an objective shot, underlining the fact that she has been vanquished, not just by one person, but by the colonial/postcolonial 'fatherly' system.

## Le jeune-homme

On the first page of the original scenario, Diouana's love interest appears as 'Le Jeune-homme' (the young man) in the list of characters. In the body of the screenplay, though, and specifically during the two flashbacks, he is listed as 'le fiancé'. Regardless of how one defines his part, he plays an important role in the film, providing Diouana with a sentimental anchor that keeps her connected to Dakar. However, he is never fully developed as a character to merit even the badge of boyfriend, and much less so that of 'fiancé'.

During the first flashback, the young man is peripheral: the two of them run into each other during Diouana's search for work, and he recommends where to go if she wants to find a nanny job. It is in the second flashback that he takes on a larger role. The flashback begins in the Place de l'Indépendance, where Diouana and the young man hold hands and go for a stroll. This is the place where the photo was taken that Diouana carries with her to France. However, during this walk Diouana becomes annoyed with the young man when he grabs her breast in public, as they pose for the photo.[31]

Ce film a obtenu
le Prix Jean VIGO 1966

Une co-production

LES ACTUALITES FRANÇAISES    Films DOMIREV
(Paris)        (Dakar)

Visa de Contrôle cinématographique N° 31.617

L A N O I R E de ...

d'après une nouvelle
de
SEMBENE Ousmane

Tirée de VOLTAIQUE - Editions Présence Africaine

avec

Mbissine Thérèse DIOP ............ La Bonne
Anne-Marie JELINCK .......... Madame
Momar Nar SENE ............. Le Jeune-homme
Robert FONTAINE ......... Monsieur

Les invités : Bernard DELBARD - Nicole DONATI
Raymond LEMERY - Suzanne LEMERY

Ibrahima BOY ............. Le Masque

Les enfants : Philippe - Sophie - Damien

Avec les voix de :
Toto BISSAINTHE
Robert MARCY
Sophie LECLERC

Images ...................... Christian LACOSTE
Assistants .................. Ibrahima BARRO
Pathé DIOP

Montage ........ André GAUDIER
LABORATOIRE C.T.M. - Gennevilliers

après la dernière image : Ecrit et Réalisé
par
SEMBENE Ousmane

(Courtesy Lilly Library, Indiana University, Bloomington, Indiana)

She walks away from him in protest, while excitedly thinking to herself that she is going to France. In other words, his behaviour does not really faze her. After they separate for a moment, Diouana returns to sit by him in the plaza and asks if he thinks France is more beautiful than here in downtown Dakar. He responds that he does not know because he has never been. Sembene cuts away from their

stilted dialogue to a man watering the lawn, a moment that deserves an extended parenthesis.

This is in fact the second time Sembene inserts a shot of a lawn being watered. On the first occasion, Diouana is in the yard at Madame's house in Dakar, and her eyes follow a sprinkler, then seen in two separate POV shots. Her gesture mimics, in effect, the rotary

movement of the sprinkler. The triple visual spotlight (once downtown, twice in the garden) on this anodyne, everyday moment signals Sembene's evocation of the first comedy in the history of cinema, Louis Lumière's *L'Arroseur arrosé/The Sprinkler Sprinkled* (1895). Lumière's film was among the very first to be introduced to the West African colonies, as early as 1900 (Thackway 2003: 7). Moreover, in the first volume of *African Cinema*, Olivier Barlet and Claude Forest provide us with an extensive list of key dates in the history of African cinemas. Among these, they specify a screening of *L'Arroseur arrosé* 'in a circus in Dakar' in 1900 (2023: 419). Similarly, Paulin Vieyra mentions the same projection in Dakar on the first page of his book *Le Cinéma africain: des origines à 1973* (1975). The introduction of Lumière's short comedy to Senegal appears to have been a foundational moment. Sembene adds his own interpretation of lawn watering in a reflexive cinematic moment that echoes the beginnings of cinema and provides us with material callback to the early movement, also rotary, of the *Cinématographe* invented by the Lumière brothers.

In contrast, the young man does not seem to show any reverence for France and is clearly upset at the news that Diouana is about to leave. Unbothered, she walks away from him, thinking to herself that his opinion (namely, that her job would amount to 'domestic slavery') does not really matter. She reminds herself in voiceover that her mother has given her permission and repeats to herself 'To France! To France!' She takes off her heels and literally hops up the steps leading to a war monument, which is revealed to have been erected to honour and show gratitude to 'our dead'

between 1939 and 1945. Françoise Pfaff identifies the places where Diouana and the young man walk as 'Dakar's center, the *Place de l'Indépendance* (Independence Square), formerly the Place Protêt, a square created by the French on the site of an old French fort erected in 1857 during the colonial conquest of Senegal' (2004: 93). Pfaff also specifies that the monument was built by the French, which complicates the symbolic interpretation of its inclusion: the grateful nation is then France, but that gratitude could only be taken with a grain of salt. Moreover, Sembene chooses to intercut the scene with archival images from a wreath-laying event. The inclusion of this documented ritual bridges the colonial and post-independence periods, (re)actualising the former in an ominous way. In doing so, Sembene vindicates Diouana's gesture and subtly criticises her date, who takes great offence and yells at her to come down because 'it's a sacrilege' (what she 'offends' is colonial memory). She obliges and they both run across the street.

Jumping forward in time, Sembene skips to their next date. The young man picks Diouana up by her house, just as she is promising her little brother that she will bring him to France. Cigarette in his mouth and *Elle* magazine in his hands, he quietly walks by her side.

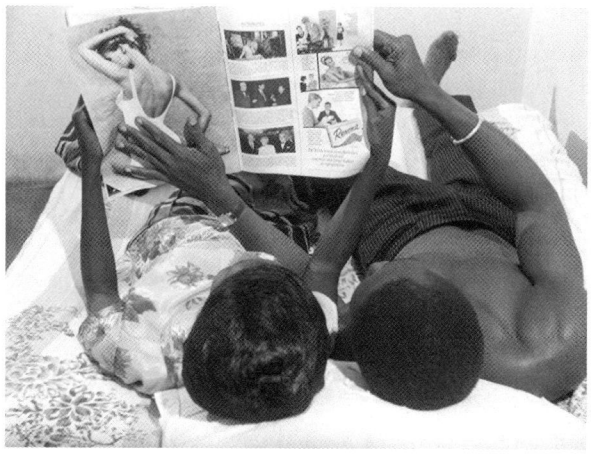

With another jump cut, we find them lying in bed, heads towards the
audience, as they both flip through the magazine. While Diouana is
fully dressed, he is half-naked and has also changed his trousers from
the previous scene. The suggestion is that we find them in a post-
coital state, but that might not explain Diouana's rhetorical question
to herself: 'Why is he sulking?' She sits up on the bed, thinking
to herself that she is already in his room, so what more could he
want? The camera cuts to the young man pouring himself a glass of
water. Behind him, a prominent cloth poster completes the decor.
It is a reversed image of Patrice Lumumba, with the words 'Congo
Indépendance' encircling his image, and the letters MNC below it.
The acronym stands for the Congolese National Movement, the
party started and led by Lumumba. The other visible word, '*uhuru*',
repeated on the cloth, is the Swahili for 'Freedom', which indicates
that the young man supports the tenets of the pan-African movement.
The camera then returns to Diouana, who smiles and takes off her
wig, followed by her top. Even though he had just lit up another
cigarette, the young man immediately puts it out and returns to bed,
his movement blurring the focus of the camera in a signal that we are
not privy to what follows.

The fact that Diouana decides to have sex with the young man, perhaps for a second time, is not in the original script.[32] If one simply reads her lines on page 16, one might only infer frustration: 'Why is he sulking? I am at his place. What more does he want? I have to go to France. I promised my boss!'[33] In commentary about the portrayal of sexuality in early African films, Françoise Pfaff identifies 'languorous love-filled gazes', which 'may convey a subdued erotic content to viewers as occurs in Ousmane Sembene's *Black Girl* ... between Diouana and her boyfriend' (1996: 254). I am not entirely certain, however, that there is any real intimacy in the exchange between the two characters. Diouana's smile as she takes off her wig could simply suggest that she has figured out what he wants (i.e. more sex), while the young man's face completely lacks any suggestion of a 'love-filled' look.

When the camera regathers its focus in its movement away from the young man's room, the narrative has transitioned back to present-day Diouana, lying on the bed in Antibes. The first visible element following the return to her own room is her bare left foot, which maintains an equivocal suggestion of the sexual moment that started off in the past. The camera swivels around the bed, revealing her

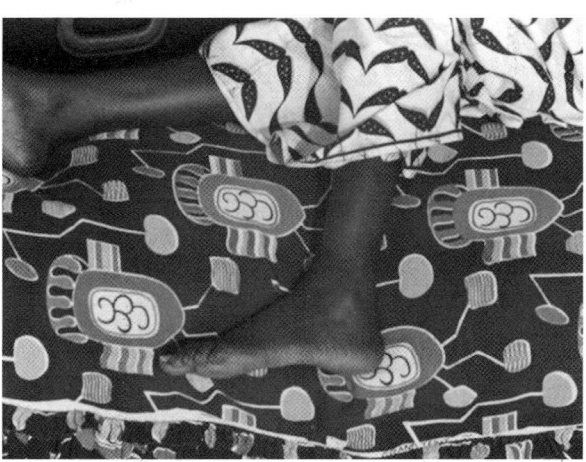

other foot, the open suitcase, Diouana sleeping, and then descends by her side, showing us the apron to the side of the bed and, finally, the mask lying on the ground. Next to the mask, there are two photos: the one taken during their stroll, only that here the mask covers up the young man so that only Diouana is visible; and a second one featuring only the young man leaning against a tree, looking away from the viewfinder, captured in a moment that Sembene's camera does not. Inside the room, the following shot keeps swivelling to find Diouana's flats, and then rises to recapture her left foot, thus closing off a very brief narrative loop. The young man is on his way to disappearing in the present day, discarded on the floor, and even erased by the covering of the photograph. His fleeting memory is not enough to keep Diouana alive.

## Sembene

Sembene makes a small but consequential appearance in the film. At the beginning of the first flashback, a blurry image that slowly becomes clearer marks the transition back in time. Memory is unreliable and 'blurry', but when the shot comes into focus, we see a young boy wearing the mask we had first observed in the apartment

in Antibes. A voice from off screen tells him to put it down, which he immediately does. This very brief acousmatic instance establishes Sembene as a godlike figure (according to Chion, the original *acousmêtre* is God; 1999: 27). The framing widens to include the source of this voice – a public letter writer, sitting at a desk outside, played by the director himself, omnipresent pipe in his mouth.

The door behind him opens and Diouana steps out. Sembene asks her where she is going, and she responds that she is looking for work. The act of interrogating his own character is a playful detail: Sembene makes it seem that he does not know where his very own character will end up!

The next time the public letter writer appears, he does so only by way of sonic inference during the reading of the letter from Diouana's mother, which logic dictates would have likely been transcribed by him (since Diouana cannot read or write in French, it would seem safe to assume that the same applied to her mother). Sembene, the character, provides us with sonic links that connect Diouana's mother to the main protagonist and, by virtue of Monsieur reading the letter out loud, also with the French couple, which brings together a total of five characters, or most of the cast. Sembene, the letter writer, interacts with Monsieur more directly when the latter returns Diouana's suitcase to Dakar. In a first instance, he points him out to the young people standing outside his office, and the camera swivels around to reveal their intense facial reactions. He then directs Monsieur towards Diouana's mother, and when she refuses the money, too, he explains to him that she does not want it.

Sembene's self-insertion in an authoritative role, as someone capable of reading and writing, as a person to whom others listen, potentially as even a godlike figure, is momentous. He presents himself as the intellectual centre of the neighbourhood, its moral centre with a dash of sententiousness, and a translator between cultures and races. In short, he is an engaged entity in a way that hints at his burgeoning real-life cultural influence, as he develops his own version of a *cinéma-engagé*, a politically charged type of film-making that foreshadows the teachings and ideology of Third Cinema (the famous Solanas/Getino manifesto appeared in 1969). We might say that this small fictional part represents the very beginnings of Sembene-as-sun metaphor. Significantly, in real life Sembene writes Diouana's history from an African point of view. His version of the story counteracts the callousness of the newspaper article that had caught his attention in the 1950s and exposes the challenges of making Diouana fully fledged in a world that constantly aims to deny her very existence. The final product represents the first in-depth filmic representation of the Black African émigré's psyche, placed in the postcolonial context that straddles both Senegal and France. Therefore, Diouana ends up as a larger-than-life character and as *the* referential point for characters from African cinemas (as proven by the fact that Sembene's film is the postcolonial visual text that has garnered by far the most academic attention in journals and books).

## The young brother

Diouana's younger brother turns up several times and almost always in connection with the mask. Diouana 'buys' the mask from him, on the unfulfilled promise that she would give him money later. He hangs around the public writer's office and walks the dusty streets of the neighbourhood. However, he becomes especially meaningful because the film concludes on his face. In the denouement, following Monsieur's unsuccessful attempt to give Diouana's mother money, the young boy picks up the mask from atop the suitcase. Mask over his face, he begins to follow Monsieur, past the office of the letter

writer, past the neighbourhood barracks, across the highway and all the way to his car. Monsieur looks back several times, and, as the scene unfolds, this gesture appears to increasingly imply that it is the mask that chases him away. The object was never just that, an object; it was always more significant: what chases Monsieur is Diouana's ghost, and along with her, the mother, and along with them, the neighbourhood, and likely also the ancestors (the ghosts of slaves).[34] So, in a sense, it is generations of Africans that finally chase the white coloniser out of the continent. Nevertheless, a more cynical reading of the moment is that Monsieur is back in Dakar not only to return Diouana's remains, but to find a replacement for her, and that could very well be Sembene's darkest metaphor for the postcolonial period, which looks set to perpetuate and repeat colonial behaviours ad infinitum.

After Monsieur gets in the car, the young brother, still wearing the mask, stares at the camera. He slowly reveals his face from behind the mask, and the film ends in a quasi-freeze-frame that radiates outwards into the extradiegetic, winking at one of the most legendary freeze-frames in world cinema, the final image of François Truffaut's *Les Quatre cents coups/The 400 Blows* (1959), which also ends on

a young man's face. The moment also radiates forwards, pointing to
the future, as Sembene's *Xala* (1974) and *Ceddo/Outsiders* (1977)
both end in proper freeze-frames. The mask represents the past, the
ancestors who are needed in order to move forward into the future,
but it also reveals the face of 'young Africa' (Vieyra 2012: 75).
Moreover, as the credits appear, Sembene Ousmane's full name is
superimposed on the young brother's face. A prophetic connection
is thus established between the youthfulness of the character and the
fact that this is Sembene's feature debut. As a result, the last frame of
the film suggests that this marks the beginning of African cinemas,
while simultaneously projecting the importance of Sembene for the
future of African cultures. Yet the fade-out that follows, while a
classic type of bookend to a film, equally invokes the uncertainty
(or darkness) of this future, too.

## **3** Objects

In addition to the mask, Sembene chose to highlight numerous other objects: Diouana's dresses, her suitcase, the photographs she carries around, the boat on which she arrives in Marseille (*Ancerville*), the poster from the young man's room and, finally, Diouana herself (with both her voice and body conceptualised as objects, dehumanised by the colonial era and the tumultuous postcolonial period that followed). Although Sembene does give her character depth (through voiceover especially), ultimately, she is still flattened by inescapable historical realities and reduced to the two-dimensionality of the newspaper article announcing her death.

### More mask
The mask comes into view early in the film, signalling its significance. After the trip from the harbour, Monsieur and Diouana enter the apartment, and Diouana notices the mask on the wall to her left.

Sembene reveals the origins of the mask in the first flashback, after we find out that Madame had picked Diouana from a large group of young women trying to find work as nannies in Dakar. Diouana had appeared rather passive and was the only one who had not thrown herself at Madame. The moment in which Madame chooses Diouana as her maid is reminiscent of 'a slave auction' according to Ukadike (1994: 77), which presages the events that will unfold in Antibes. Elated that she has been chosen and given a job as a nanny, Diouana runs home. She comes across her little brother and picks up the mask from him; meeting a female friend, or perhaps a relative, carrying a bucket of water, Diouana circles around her, holding the mask to her face, repeating that she has a job 'with white folks'. She also lets the public letter writer know the news, belatedly responding to his earlier query. Finally, she arrives home and tells her mother. When her young brother tries to reclaim the mask, Diouana purchases it from him on credit, promising to give him fifty francs at the end of the month.

The next day, when she arrives at Madame's home in Dakar, Diouana gifts her the mask. When Monsieur emerges, the wife shows him the gift, and he declares, 'Looks like the real thing'. The Criterion subtitles omit a key word that he uses in French,

'*il à l'air authentique*' (it seems authentic), which is a thorny term in postcolonial studies (that is, who decides what is authentic, and for whom?).[35] Monsieur looks around the apartment, searching for a spot for the new mask. Two other masks are shown in POV shots, indicating that Monsieur and Madame had already received such gifts, or that perhaps they had purchased them. There are smaller wooden statuettes on the shelf where Monsieur decides to put the mask, and in the middle of the frame a cloth painting of an African woman carrying a water bucket atop her head. The year marked on the lower left corner of the painting, 1962, establishes that the couple's 'collecting' extends several years into the past.[36]

Monsieur sits down and the couple, seated on either side of the object, looks intently towards the mask. Sembene shows the mask in the reverse shot by way of another POV, which, given the angle, belongs to Monsieur. Next to it, a small fertility statue is also visible. The POV shots are crucial to the reading of the scene and of the objects around the apartment, as they establish a pattern of agency on the part of Monsieur (and, by extension, of the couple) – the audience mediates and experiences these objects through their (faulty) perspective. In other words, the couple decides what is 'authentic'. They control the scopic gaze, and in the process the mask initially loses its ancestral powers. Olivier Barlet refers to the mask as Sembene's way of tracing an itinerary 'signifying the cruelty of contempt' ('*pour signifier la cruauté du mépris*') (1996: 170). It is unclear whose contempt he means, but perhaps the mask serves a dual purpose: the contempt of Africans towards colonial plunder, and the contempt of Monsieur, as a representative of the colonisers, towards the cultural production of the continent, which he reduces to a selective collection. Regardless, it is immediately clear that this object plays an important role and, indeed, Sembene uses it to move the plot forward. One could think of the mask as the opposite of the MacGuffin – this is a meaningful object *and* a known quantity, around which the entire film revolves.[37] Moreover, once it changes hands, from the brother to Diouana to Monsieur, the goal becomes its recapturing (Diouana from the couple, and the brother from Diouana).

This is exactly what Diouana does, after refusing to work. She takes the mask off the wall, brings it into her bedroom, sits down next to it and thinks back on her decision to leave Dakar. Her head moves back and forth as she stares at the ceiling, and the camera follows the logic of her eyeline, moving back and forth, too, across the white paint. In many instances when Sembene affords Diouana a point of view, they seem to be pointless. Case in point, she appears to be literally watching paint dry. Since agency and point of view are denied her, Diouana travels back in time again. The second flashback begins with a shot of a street plaque marking 'Place de l'Indépendance', in downtown Dakar. Beginning the episode here represents quite the ironic turn, since the temporal jump moves from an interior space that is hardly indicative of independence (i.e. Diouana's room/prison) to an outdoor location literally named 'Independence'. However, it may be that reclaiming the object grants her the power to manipulate time and space inside the fictional world of the film. In the additional features for the Criterion edition, Manthia Diawara explains that masks are often connected to an

African god and he interprets Diouana's gift as giving her gods away
to white people. In Diawara's documentary, Sembene admits that
'I could've ended the film with her death, but I wanted to explore the
mythical element of the child with the mask.' The mythical quality
dissipates once the object changes hands, but the narrative arc of
the film brings Diouana to the realisation of her error, followed by
her attempts to reclaim the object, along with reimbuing it with
ancestral attributes. What she takes back during the argument with
Madame is no longer a simple object, but a gateway back home by
way of the realm of deities. In the end, what kills Diouana, according
to Vieyra, is being removed from her community: 'The suicide [...]
could only occur because the individual found herself outside of the
lively community' (1975: 164).[38] Although she cannot rejoin that
community, the mask might grant her access to an equally important
community – that of the ancestors.

    To close, it is worth pointing out that on a literal level the mask
has a gaping mouth, but, naturally, it cannot speak. However, its
'voice' is channelled through Diouana, who, in a sense, makes the
mask come to life. Throughout the film, there seems to be a back-and-
forth dialogue between the character and the mask, her only friend

and interlocutor. The mask, as a signifier for the continent and as a reminder of its 'different faces' (ibid.: 163–4), or as a 'symbol for Africa' (Vieyra 2012: 75), transfers its ancestral powers to Diouana. In turn, Diouana renders the mask alive by lending it her own voice, which briefly inhabits the wooden face. The connection between Diouana and the mask may also alleviate one of my personal gripes with the denouement of the film and the common reading of her death as 'resistance'. Under this new interpretation, Diouana only dies in the traditional, Global North understanding of the process. The mask returns to Dakar and thus, along with it, Diouana's soul is reunited with the past, the ancestors and with the future, thanks to her brother holding it in the last frame of the film. If there is an underlying message of resistance, it is less so in the act of killing herself. Instead, it rather materialises from the communion between character and object, both bringing to light ancestral beliefs.

## The boat

As the action fades in, the first visible object on screen is the boat, *Ancerville*, on which Diouana arrives in Marseille. The boat slowly moves from left to right, its horn letting everyone know of its arrival.

In the second shot, Sembene pans from the opposite direction, right to left, starting with the faint outline of the Basilica of Notre-Dame de la Garde – one of the major symbols of the city – and then returning to the boat on the left of the frame. The opposite movements of the action and the camera create an effect of closure – the arrival is a contained event. The screen goes to black and the credits roll, as the horn of the *Ancerville* sounds off again. At one level, the sonic intrusion of the horn complements the visual cue of the boat. At another level, the sound could be interpreted as a warning, not just for the passengers and the harbour workers, but for the spectators, too (i.e. 'pay attention, terrible things are about to happen').

A couple of shots that focus on people working on the dock follow, which have a special resonance given Sembene's own experience as a docker and his novel *Black Docker*. Then the camera returns to the boat, revealing its name, as passengers stand on the bow. A gangway swings from left to right above the camera, connecting the boat with the shore. In the next shot, the audience meets the main character, walking from right to left, the click-clack of her shoes conspicuously audible. Even though unseen, her shoes are made visible by this sonic interjection, which also helps draw the attention of the spectators to the fact that Diouana wears a chic outfit: white headscarf, white sundial earrings, a white necklace, a white dress with black polka dots, a suitcase in her right hand and a handbag in her left. Just as he does with the first two shots of the film, Sembene continues to play with directions, matching up movements going into opposite directions and seemingly towards one another. The result of this editorial collision of sorts anticipates the clashes that will unfold throughout the film.

After Diouana crosses the gangway, Sembene frames her in a medium close-up. She swivels her head back and forth, and her voiceover comes in for the first time: 'Will someone be waiting for me?' The wind blows the ends of her white scarf – a kind of anticipatory capitulation. The boat, if considered only within the economy of the film, is not all that significant. It is simply the means of transport that

brings Diouana to France. However, it garners additional meanings when considered in conjunction with Mambety's character Anta from *Touki Bouki*, who also makes the journey by boat to France. In fact, Anta's colourful outfit also features a scarf, tied around her red hat, which constantly blows in the Dakarois wind. The stakes are different in Mambety's film because its denouement finds the two lovers, Anta and Mory, on the brink of separation, and indeed, only Anta decides to make the same journey as Diouana. The point is that this boat is a constitutive part of the common psyche of the Senegalese people, much like Gorée Island. Also akin to Gorée, postcolonial filmic references to boats may conjure up gruesome images of the transatlantic slave trade. While the African directors underline the fact that Diouana and Anta get on this boat willingly, they also indicate that the end results might not be all that dissimilar. Given what happens to Diouana, there is no sense in imagining a better outcome for Anta.[39]

### The suitcase
As she walks into the harbour, Diouana puts the suitcase on a bench on which the word '*sud*' is scribbled in chalk, presumably indicating the boat's arrival in the South of France. An officer draws the letter L

on the corner of the suitcase, which seems to be some kind of customs marker. At the end of the car ride with Monsieur, the same L is visible once again as Diouana picks up the suitcase from the pavement, next to the parked car. She looks up towards the top of the building, the camera lingering on her face, as she seems *transportée* in thought, imagining the wonders of the apartment. The audience learns much

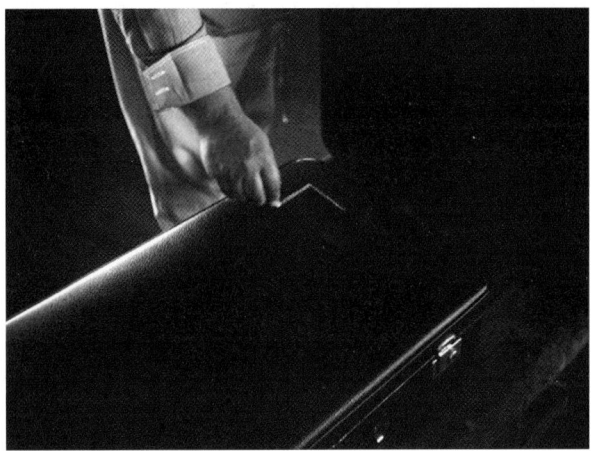

later that it was Madame who gave her dresses and a suitcase, presumably in preparation for her departure to France, which renders their meanings more complex. Sarah Gamalinda offers the intriguing possibility that the suitcase, made of leather, is a veritable skin that acts like a stand-in for Diouana herself:

the black leather suitcase and its metonymic relation to Diouana of black skin and a hollowed container. [...] Diouana faces a similar horror of finding herself akin to the objects trapped inside the suitcase and the black leather box itself, skin stretched over a hollow frame. (2022: 54)

Indeed, Diouana's entire life fits inside this object. Her clothes make up the bulk of her belongings, but the suitcase also contains her memories. The immateriality of memory becomes tangible when considering that, on occasion, she takes out the photograph with the young man.

While reading the suitcase as a surrogate for Diouana is a compelling interpretation, it could also be thought of as a coffin – akin to the sonic shell from Chapter 1 – inside which Monsieur brings her home. In other words, the gift of the suitcase is in essence the gift of death. Before Diouana kills herself, Sembene also shows her being very deliberate about packing her suitcase neatly. Why would she spend so much time and afford all this attention to the packing of the suitcase? One possible explanation is that the decision to kill herself occurs after packing the suitcase. However, Diouana's voiceover also repeatedly lets us know that several actions would 'never again' happen, including that Madame would never again lie to her or abuse her.[40] In this light, organising the suitcase represents a kind of ritual of death and self-mourning. Inside the pseudo-coffin she places her most cherished memory (the photograph) and her favourite dress (in which she would be metaphorically buried, akin to the typical white linen cloth that envelops the dead body in the Muslim tradition[41]). To be sure, Sembene places the suitcase and mask together in the same shot, following the discovery of the horror in the bathroom. The cutaway to the suitcase, mask still atop, points to Diouana's disappearance inside the object, which waits to be picked up by Monsieur (see p. 60). Following the logic of this reading, what Monsieur returns home are Diouana's earthly remains, inside the makeshift coffin, and her soul, in the form of the mask, which hovers over the physical remains.

Following the gruesome scene in the bathroom, Sembene completely changes registers by taking the audience out of the apartment and to the sunny beaches of Antibes. Furthermore, he superimposes the sound of a cheerful piano, the same piano hall music that played during the arrival sequence. Women are sunning themselves and children are frolicking in the sand. A random man reads *Nice-Matin*. He opens up the paper and under '*Les faits divers*', we can read a version of the title that is already familiar to us from the short story, '*À Antibes, une jeune négresse se tranche la gorge dans la salle de bains de ses patrons*' (In Antibes, a young Black woman cuts her own throat in her employers' bathroom). One cannot help but think that the indifferent title reveals a certain level of annoyance, as if Diouana violated the rights of her bosses by taking this action in *their* bathroom.

The next shot returns to the apartment, where we find Madame ostensibly upset at the news. As she lights up a cigarette, the shot widens to reveal Monsieur reading the same newspaper as the man on the beach. He looks at Madame, then says that they are to go back to Dakar. Madame goes to the bathroom, takes Diouana's housecoat off the wall and then looks down. In the reverse shot, we see a sparkling, clean bathtub – any trace of the horror has been removed. However, in the very next shot, the mask reappears in a close-up, reminding us that Diouana's presence, or soul, transcends the wiped traces of blood from the tub. Monsieur picks up the mask and the suitcase, then stops to collect the housecoat that Madame brings to him. He places the suitcase on the floor and opens it, seemingly surprised to see the photograph on the top. A very generous reading of his gestures, and overall behaviour, is that he belatedly realises that Diouana was a human being, with her own dreams, aspirations and loves.

### The photograph

The photograph that elicits a reaction from the stoic Monsieur is another notable object. The audience first gets a good look at the photograph inside Diouana's room. She has just let the sun in by

raising the blinds. The camera follows Diouana from outside
looking in, and the character is caught between the frames of the
window. The right side of the frame is almost completely obscured,
creating an obvious contrast with the left side. She opens the other
half of the window and steps forward to look out inquisitively.
Once again, Sembene denies her (and the audience) the reverse
POV shot. She walks back into the room, opens her suitcase and
looks at the photograph inside. Following a cutaway shot back to
Madame cleaning up after herself (the horror!), the action returns
to Diouana's room, as Sembene places the camera right behind her
left shoulder.

Diouana is holding the photograph, clearly maintaining contact
with a precious memory. In the photograph, she wears a striped dress,
a small corner of which is also discernible inside the suitcase, linking
past and present by way of a material item. We can also see the young
man from Dakar, his left arm draped around her. She is looking
off frame (of the photograph), once again *transportée* (or perhaps
distracted), while he is looking at her. The last chapter revisits the
multiple visual frames that Sembene employs throughout the film, but
it is important to pause here and underline the game of visual frames,
previously introduced by the intradiegetic frames of the windows.
The Diouana of the present, back towards us, stands opposite the
frame of the window jamb and bisected by the frame of the camera.
The Diouana of the past finds herself first framed by the margins
of the photograph, then a second time by the rectangular suitcase,
then by the window jamb and present Diouana, and finally by the
frame of the camera. Moreover, the Diouana of the past is 'framed'
by temporality, seemingly frozen in a past moment. Then again, in
André Bazin's words, the photograph 'embalms time', but its object is
'freed from the conditions of time and space' (1971: 14). As we have
already discovered, Diouana indeed travels back and forth between
past and present.[42]

To ensure that the spectators pay attention to the meanings of
these multiple frames, Sembene doubles down on the game and has

Diouana carefully re-place the photograph inside the top part of the suitcase, creating a series of connected rectangular shapes (a memory trapped in the suitcase, and then further trapped within the cinematic frame). Following this gesture, she then takes out the striped dress and, carefully still, places the photograph back inside the suitcase, which she closes. The chalk L from customs is still there, reminding us that only a short period of time has elapsed. Bazin also refers to the art of photography as being akin to the process of mummification – an attempt to stall the passage of time (ibid.: 9–11). The multiple frames, or layers, that constantly drape Diouana, whether as represented by the film or as represented by the photograph *within* the representation of the film, could well be construed as Sembene's attempt to preserve this character infinitely.

## Promotional poster and dresses

It makes sense to bundle these objects together under one category, because Diouana wears one of her two elegant dresses – the striped one – on the promotional poster for the film. Moreover, it is with this film that Sembene developed a penchant for showcasing meaningful intradiegetic posters. Diouana arrives in Marseille wearing her best

Sunday outfit, a polka-dot dress, complete with striking jewellery and carefully coiffed wig. The fact that the outfits are gifts from Madame poses a challenge to one of the common readings of Diouana's refusal to take off the elegant dress while she cleans the kitchen and bathroom (yet again, she 'resists'). Certainly, her refusal to remove the white dress with vertical black lines could be construed as an act of rebellion. Yet, and perhaps more importantly, the gesture also connotes a depressing irony, because the dress, already suggestive of prison bars, becomes a de facto prison/kitchen uniform.

The promotional poster for the film, showing Diouana in the striped dress, is visible in a clever shot from Sembene's *Xala*. In the last scene of this film, El Hadji's son comes out of his room to see what the ruckus is about, then makes a deliberate gesture to open the door wider. In the background, one can clearly see the extradiegetic poster of *Black Girl*, which in this case is also intradiegetic. This choice could be taken as a self-reflexive nod, as the director briefly returns to his first feature-length film; it could also serve as a reminder to the audience that he is an award-winning director, because the poster lists all the awards; finally, it could be, of course, self-advertisement.[43] Nevertheless, it is its appearance as a prop that renders the promotional poster for *Black Girl* (normally

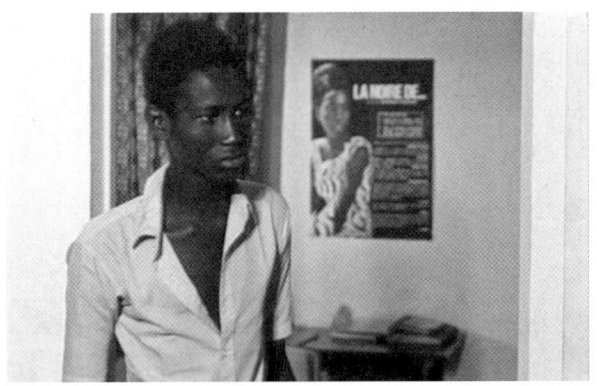

*Xala* (1974)

not connected with the reading of the film, as it sits outside those confines) an *object* worthy of inclusion in this section.

Generally speaking, a poster on a wall fuctions as a *mise-en-scène* prop that generates a reciprocal connection between the world of the film and the real world, imbuing it with a double semiotic value: what it signifies in the economy of the film, and what it means for the larger socio-cultural context. For example, at the diegetic level, the cloth poster of Lumumba in the young man's room gives us an indication of his political leanings. In the African cinescape, the larger context almost always has to do with identifying postcolonial tensions, supporting the continued fight for independence or restating pan-African principles. In fact, numerous posters chosen by Sembene carry an element of nostalgia, as they look to the past for both remembrance and inspiration towards a pan-African future. To illustrate, the character Rama from Sembene's *Xala* has posters of pan-African heroes Amílcar Cabral and Samori Touré, but also of Charlie Chaplin (visible on p. 12).[44] Moreover, on Rama's door, a small colour poster of Sembene's *Mandabi* is visible for a split second, as James S. Williams observes (2024: 98). Decades later, the title character from *Faat Kiné* adorns the walls of her home with life-sized portraits of other political figures, such as Nelson Mandela and Kwame Nkrumah. The motif of the poster travels across several films (and to other film-makers), thus creating an extradiegetic narrative that amounts to a virtual tapestry of colonial and postcolonial struggles.

To return to Diouana, the dress from the poster also appears in the flashback sequences. If in France the striped dress functions as an additional reminder of her imprisonment, in Dakar it is a reminder of simpler, more light-hearted times, although one can still make the argument that Diouana is trapped in her own memory, and therefore still a prisoner of sorts. On the poster, an absent-minded Diouana gazes off screen as she often does in the film and the short story. More importantly, her mouth is slightly open, in a Mona Lisa-like ambiguous smile. This extradiegetically connects the character from the poster with the most important object in the film, the mask, which also has an open mouth.

## Body as object

It is perhaps already clear that the film potentially turns Diouana into an object. Her employers and other white characters objectify her. Sembene, too, transfers much of her essence into meaningful objects (suitcase and mask), but he does so to help her transcend the physical body and to turn her into an enduring metaphor for the postcolonial subject. However, he also films Diouana's body in an ambiguous manner that could be construed as objectifying. After the key scene during which Diouana walks around the apartment, looking first at the mask and then into the darkness of the night, she gets ready for bed. Patiently waiting for the character to take off all her clothes, Sembene's camera frames almost her entire body, as the shot changes into a long take. Referencing this moment, Françoise Pfaff finds 'highly erotic connotations' in the 'prolonged shot of a naked body' (1996: 255). Although granted there is a voyeuristic element to the shot, the intradiegetic male agent through whom the audience could channel their voyeurism is missing from this sequence.

Therefore, the prolonged shot might have more to do with increasing and emphasising Diouana's loneliness. If one were to counterpoint two scenes – Diouana and the young man in his bedroom, and Diouana taking off her clothes alone – the point of isolation becomes even clearer.

Nevertheless, there is no question that the scene is paradoxical. On the one hand, the paradox stems from the reality of watching a woman strip down to her underwear in what amounts to clear-cut objectification. On the other, Sembene possibly minimises the suggestion of lasciviousness. The reduced voyeuristic effect comes from the fact that, as Diouana undresses, she simultaneously continues to reveal herself sonically, slowly peeling away the layers of the reality she faces. In other words, Sembene directs the audience's attention away from the naked body and towards the sonic version of Diouana, which, incidentally, also bares herself. As she reaches the conclusion that she is alone and wonders about whether this is all there is to France, she slips into bed and the scene closes with a fade-out, the symbolic black hole that swallows up both her sonic and visual bodies.

# 4 Visual Frames: Where It Ends

Before returning to the key moment of the film (Diouana's face-to-face with the mask), we begin where the last chapter ended – on transitions. Although Sembene makes effective use of the fade-out, an even more evocative transition is the right-to-left wipe effect. After Madame shows Diouana her room for the first time, she immediately tells her, 'Now let's go and see the kitchen.' Following their exit from the bedroom, Sembene transitions via a right-to-left wipe to Diouana, wiping the bathtub. In a prophetic first act as a housekeeper, she cleans the bathtub in which the ending of the film will find her dead. From the tub, she moves to the mirror, which she vigorously wipes. Her reflection is a more traditional visual dedoubling of the character in comparison with the multi-split brought about by shadows, mask and sonic presence. The classic interpretation of diegetic mirrors is that they point to dualities, such as reality vs. fantasy, or to a character having two sides. In Diouana's case, the

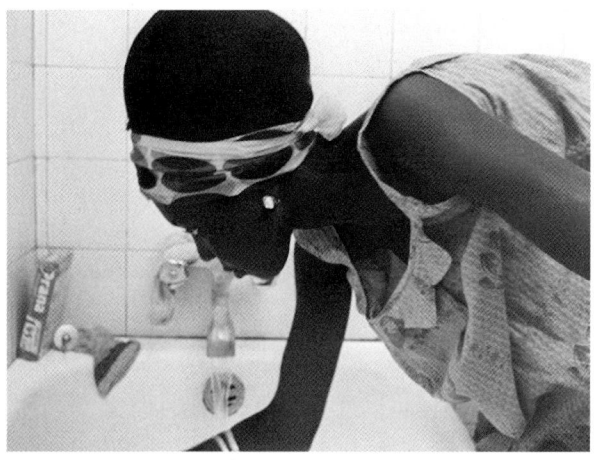

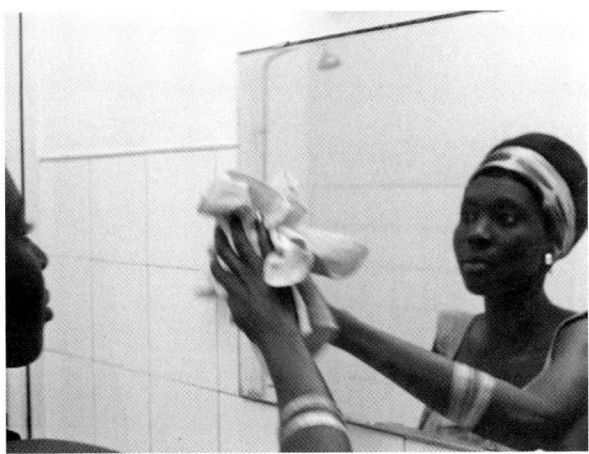

cinematic combination of a wipe effect followed by a reflection that the character literally tries to wipe off suggests the figurative erasure of what she had imagined about France – things are hardly as they seem. What is certain is that the mirror functions like a second frame, inside the regular frame of the camera, which captures (pun intended) Diouana. No matter how much she wipes, she is trapped inside this version of the reflection – Diouana, the disillusioned maid.

After cleaning the bathroom, Diouana goes back to her room and makes the bed. The camera patiently waits for her to finish tidying up, then to put her earrings and jewellery back on. It is another obstinate act of defiance, like wearing the elegant dress, because in the next shot (accessed via another right-to-left wipe), she is back in the kitchen washing dishes. After she hangs up the laundry to dry, she begins to wash the floors. The floor pattern alternates carceral black and white stripes, over which Diouana bends in her white polka-dot dress. On cue, Madame walks in to complain that Diouana has not changed out of her 'party' dress for three weeks. This is the first indication that time has elapsed, and the audience fills in the blanks, belatedly realising that Diouana has been stuck in this repetitive work cycle for weeks.

Another item of Diouana's ensemble deserves further attention, because it connects with the motif of intradiegetic frames – her shoes. As the film approaches its conclusion, Diouana walks one morning from her room to the living room. Once again, she has put on the full ensemble, black heels included. The camera tracks her movements, focusing only on her feet and shoes. When she enters the living

room, Madame stops her and demands that she remove her shoes, a reminder that she is a maid. Diouana takes them off and leaves them in the living room, then slowly walks to the kitchen, where she sits at the table. The camera again tracks her bare feet across the apartment and settles on them under the table. Following a close-up of the discarded heels, Madame enters the shot, picks them up, brings them into the kitchen and drops them by Diouana. The next shot is an

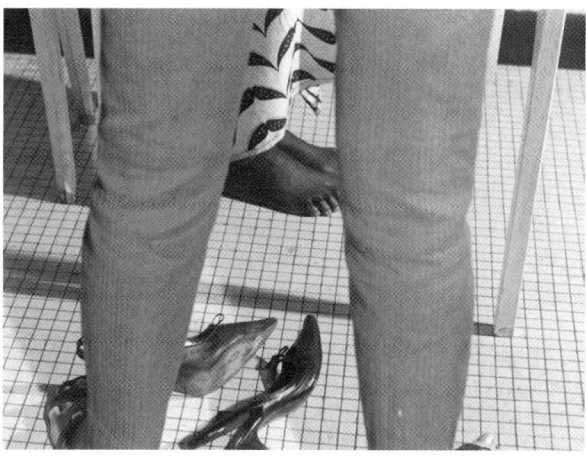

exquisite example of Sembene's artistry: Madame's legs in the foreground form a triangle through which the shoes are visible and, further up, Diouana's bare feet complete a second diegetic triangle.[45] Madame's legs, the shoes, which used to belong to Madame, and Diouana's feet enter a visual game of multiple frames. In addition to the triangle of interconnected elements, one must take into consideration the legs of the table and chair, the straight shadow that crosses the shot horizontally and Diouana's striped dress. As a result, more restrictive frames ensue – Madame's legs, the legs of the furniture, the horizontal shadow, the dress lines and, of course, the actual frame of the camera. Notably, they all surround Diouana's bare feet. There is no escape from this situation.

The theme of no escape is also discernible in the key scene first discussed in Chapter 1. In order to complete the initial sonic analysis of Diouana's voiceover, the focus of this chapter now shifts to the visual elements of the scene and its multiple intradiegetic frames. From the ambiguous shot of Monsieur passed out on his bed, the film's narrative attention returns to Diouana, whose presence brackets the insertion of Monsieur (that is, the logic of the narrative moves from Diouana cleaning the kitchen, to Monsieur sleeping, then back to Diouana, who, having finished the chores, muses about the current condition of her life in France). As Diouana moves slightly to her left, the camera tracks her from behind. However, Sembene first positions the character between the mask on the wall and a very pronounced shadow to her right, which is the result of placing the key light to the left of Diouana. Eventually, the fill light coming in from the right side will project a fainter shadow on the left of the frame. The two-point lighting generates several versions of the character on the makeshift screen (the wall), which contributes to the creation of an overall moody atmosphere.

The moody aesthetic matches Diouana's dysphoric state of mind. In voiceover, she wonders what the people back home would think of her. As she imagines what they would say, she very deliberately places her palms on the wall, on either side of

the mask, staring at it intently. One of the goals of the scene is to communicate to the audience that the character is stuck in this situation. Throughout the film, precise cinematography repeatedly underlines the condition of being trapped. It is worth repeating that Diouana's body appears to be caught between the mask and her own deep shadow. Moreover, the pronounced vertical line of the closed door further limits the cinematic space in which she can operate. Finally, the mask itself – a symbol for Senegal, but also for Diouana – is initially bracketed by the character's hands (see p. 23). The *mise en scène* is purposely sparse: the mask is the sole prop on the wall, marooned in a sea of pale, much like Diouana's own position in the apartment and as an employee of the white family.

Diouana looks back over her left shoulder, to nowhere in particular, and the reverse shot is not revealed to the audience. However, this choice has less to do with practices of experimental cinema (e.g. denying the audience the reverse shot to create distanciation and generate anxiety). Instead, and to reiterate an earlier point, Sembene signals that her perspective is less relevant, which forces the audience to follow her sonic train of thought. As she moves away from the mask, the second projected shadow on the

left comes into sharper focus, although still considerably less defined than its companion on the right. Visually, Diouana splits into three versions of herself, progressing from a hint of an outline on the wall, to the visualised body and finally to the deep shadow. To these we can add the sonic version of Diouana, and it becomes clear that we are witnessing a crisis of identity. Not so much because she does not know who she is, but because she has begun to accept having less control over her own life. One more fantastic visual detail is worth pointing out: as the character turns her head to the left, she no longer faces the mask; however, its deep shadow projected on the wall perfectly plays against Diouana's real profile. Their noses almost touching, the shadow of the mask turns into a piece of the puzzle that is meant to complete the visual Diouana. The mask is part of her, and vice versa, bringing together ancestry and present.

As she continues to walk towards the left of the frame, Diouana looks back towards the inside of the apartment. She enumerates its various rooms, which for her make up the entirety of France. Even though Diouana is mostly on the move, and even though she is almost out of the frame, Sembene still places her between restricting elements of the *mise en scène*: the electrical wall outlet to her right (as she turns towards the audience) and the trailing deep shadow to her left, which slightly overlaps with the mask and its own shadow. The game of frames quickly turns ominous, repeatedly capturing the character and squeezing her between elements from her surroundings.

Two pans to the left follow Diouana's exit to the left of the frame, thus creating a smooth rhythmic pattern (in contrast with the beginning of the film, which stresses opposing movements). From the wall of the apartment, the perspective shifts to a Stygian shot of Antibes, various lights flickering in the darkness (see p. 25). This panning shot could be from her point of view, but we never actually see Diouana looking out of an open window. Instead, Sembene cuts to the character standing once again with her back towards the audience and looking out of a closed window. The audience could assume that Diouana had opened and then shut the window, which would imply a short jump in narrative time. However, the more logical interpretation is that Sembene continues to deny her a visual point of view in order to emphasise her lack of agency. Diouana turns around again, and the motion coordinates with her previous gesture in front of the mask. Yet, in this second instance, Diouana briefly looks straight into the camera, breaking the fourth wall. The game of

frames continues, as Diouana finds herself in between three white vertical lines provided by the big windows. The alternation of white lines and black rectangles matches up with the black and white lines on the floor she has just cleaned. No matter where she is in the apartment, Diouana is a prisoner. As she exits the frame, the camera lingers for a moment on the closed windows: there is nowhere to go.

The next morning, when Madame awakens Diouana, Sembene does include two POV shots from Diouana's perspective. They are both of a histrionic Madame, standing over the bed, framed from a low angle and filmed with a handheld camera meant to correspond with Diouana's head movements. Madame supplements her aggressive actions by twice yelling 'We are not in Africa' and calling Diouana 'lazy bones'. This represents the type of point of view that Sembene permits Diouana to have – the white imperialist berating and reigning over her. The suggestion that one can be 'lazy' in Africa but not in France is nonsensical, naturally. Madame's words emphasise the fact that location does not affect the level of power exerted by the white French occupiers. Whether in Dakar or Antibes, subservience is expected.

The next visual frame worth analysing takes place in the bathroom, as Diouana combs her hair in the mirror, her left side

turned towards the camera. We do not see her reflection in the main mirror, but Sembene places a second smaller mirror on the wall to her right, which reflects the right side of her face. As a result, Diouana's full face is reconstructed in an ingenious way. To continue with the motif of restrictive intradiegetic frames, the director places the character between these two mirrors, themselves capable of further framing or reframing the reflected subject. Furthermore, the second mirror is itself reflected in the bigger mirror, creating a *mise-en-abyme* effect. Madame interrupts Diouana's morning ritual by knocking aggressively on the bathroom door. In reaction, Diouana leans back against the door and looks upward, biting her lip in frustration. A close-up of her distraught face follows, underlining the physical and psychological effects of Madame's harassment. Madame's loud banging and demands for Diouana to come out of the bathroom wake up Monsieur, who emerges from the bedroom in his pyjamas. He must have woken up from his drunken stupor and changed clothes in the middle of the night (to remind us, he passes out in his daywear). Monsieur does not respond to his wife's belligerence. He pensively strokes his chin, then exits to the right, Madame in tow, still yelling. In the next shot, the spatial perspective shifts back to

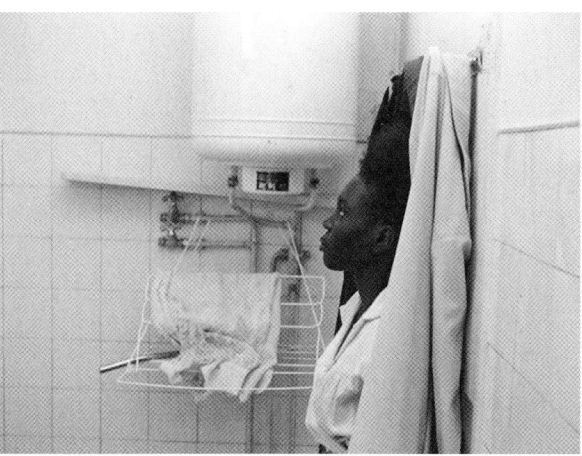

the bathroom, where we find Diouana still up against the door, but framed from the left side of her body. Her head juts out, in contrast with the white surroundings – walls, water heater, clothes rack, bathrobe and her own white shirt. As the couple drinks coffee, which Madame had to make herself – the horror, yet again – Monsieur suggests that perhaps Diouana could benefit from a break and might enjoy visiting the town. Madame maintains her solipsistic streak by opposing the idea because she is 'responsible for her'. At that exact moment, Diouana walks past them and back into her room without a word.

Her silence continues during the reading of the letter she has received and whose origin she doubts. Given this silence, it seems almost as if Diouana is being force-fed the French words and asked to accept them as the truth (or, to keep them down, as it were). The use of French in this seemingly innocuous context turns self-reflexive because of Sembene's requirement to shoot the film in the language of the coloniser (as a condition of financing). While Monsieur reads the letter out loud, the camera shifts from Madame agreeing with its tone to a shot of Diouana, likely from Madame's point of view. A vase with extravagantly fuzzy branches sits on the table, so when the

camera finds Diouana, she is doubly framed by the flowers, on either side of the close-up. The same shot structure is repeated two more times to show Madame listening intently and Monsieur throwing Diouana a look of contempt. By virtually repeating the same shot (alternating close-ups accompanied by branches), Sembene generates a cinematic showdown between the three characters, which also represents the preamble to Diouana's revolt.

## The colour scene

In the most commonly circulated version of *Black Girl*, the entire film is in black and white. Accompanying this version, the Criterion Collection edition of the film includes among its special features a short scene in colour (and not multiple scenes, as Sembene had indicated to Guy Hennebelle). The Criterion booklet explains that the BFI restored the colour sequence by using an original 35mm print preserved at their archives. When Hennebelle pressed the film-maker about the versions that are still in circulation, Sembene explained that colour remains in certain versions, including one in which 'at the beginning of her stay in Antibes, the girl saw all in pink' (2008: 10). I do not take this comment to mean, literally, that a pink filter was employed, but that using colour during the driving sequence is an ingenious way to show Diouana's state of mind upon arrival. Tobias Warner reads the scene along similar lines: 'The color sequence would then represent the "rose colored glasses" through which Diouana sees France' (2017: 119). Among their references to *Black Girl*, Murphy and Williams explain the use of colour as follows: 'her arrival in France sees the film shift from black-and-white to colour as she enters the land of her dreams' (2007: 52). They do not refer to this scene as being an extradiegetic remnant, which indicates that they are commenting on the BFI version of the original 35mm print. Even though this scene is not included in the most widespread version of the film, its existence cannot be ignored. Since the current chapter concerns itself with frames, it made sense to me to address it belatedly and in the context of the black-and-white portions of the film flanking (or framing) the short colour scene.

We return to Marseille, as Monsieur waits outside, then walks towards the arriving Diouana to help her with the suitcase. He wears a suit and sunglasses – the same ones he would later wear during the return trip to Dakar. If in the latter case, the sunglasses act as a protector from the inquisitive looks of the locals and of the mask on the young brother's face, here the sunglasses take on the more traditional cinematic value of obscuring Monsieur's face and thus making him inscrutable.[46] The action moves inside the car, with the camera initially tracking Diouana from the backseat. Monsieur asks Diouana if she had a nice trip, and from his face framed in a close-up, the perspective shifts to a POV shot of the street, suddenly in colour. As if prompted by the change, Monsieur comments that 'France is beautiful', to which Diouana finally responds with her first diegetic words: 'Yes, sir.' Importantly, the perspective belongs to Diouana, as the shots in colour are taken from the passenger seat. As this is one of the few instances when the main character is afforded a point of view, it becomes memorable in retrospect. However, this is also somewhat of a problematic POV, because the colour enhances the

brightness of the sun and the splendour of the French Riviera, thus elevating the fantasy aspect of the moment. As the car enters the city of Antibes, the film reverts to black and white well before arriving at the apartment. The short-lived fantasy passes in a flash. The colour scene is merely other people's reality and cannot belong to Diouana.

## Visual reflections

The following concluding section looks at the film's legacy, both in terms of Sembene's subsequent works, which might carry a visual trace connecting them back to *Black Girl*, and in terms of other African and African diasporic film-makers who could be in a cross-generational dialogue with Sembene. To put this another way, the aim is to explore to what extent *Black Girl* and Sembene together turn into an African cultural nucleus, or, to return to the metaphor from the introduction, a sun. Throughout the book, there have been sporadic references to world cinema, such as Lumière's first comedy, De Sica's *Bicycle Thieves*, Truffaut's *The 400 Blows* or Kurosawa's *Rashomon* (1950). However, these are largely connections radiating outwards, and it would be worth looking at several other connections that echo and radiate backwards towards *Black Girl*.

Regarding Sembene himself, the settings, the lessons and the shadows of *Black Girl* would become staples of his ensuing work. For example, when Diouana walks by a group of three fashionably dressed young men leaving the National Assembly building discussing politics, she hears them express the thought that 'For me, the future is Black.' Similar commentary (along with the well-known criticism of President Senghor) appears in *Xala*. Another visual echo with *Xala* materialises via a scene in a lift. During her search for a job, Diouana ends up in an apartment block, where she takes the lift with a young man, whom she would soon date. Alone in the same lift on her way down, Diouana stares at the flickering lights between floors. The POV shot of alternating light and darkness is a neat materialisation of the cinematic act (i.e. 'rolling' frames), which complements the shots of the rotary sprinkler. Sembene revisits a similar concept in *Xala* but focuses more on truncated reflections and optical illusions that show only parts of El Hadji's body, and not his face, to presage the character's downfall.[47] In opposition to these two examples, Sembene also uses meticulous shot composition to allude to the ability of a character to exceed the limitations of the cinematic frame. For example, both Rama in

*Xala* (1974)

*Xala* and Faat in *Faat Kiné* are symbols of a hopeful African future. Having both learned important lessons from Diouana's trials and tribulations, the two of them, Rama and Faat, reject the French fantasy that tricks Diouana.[48]

While Sembene is clearly critical of postcolonialism, he also uses Diouana's story as a warning against the naiveté of wannabe émigrés. Paulin Vieyra notes that the 'apparent simplicity' of the story 'hides the depth of the author's reflection about the social condition in Africa and the drama that Africa has to face' in the postcolonial era (1975: 162).[49] However, like the narrator from the short story, he also digresses in the odd parenthetical commentary about the 'good' conditions in which Diouana finds herself in France (i.e. she has a comfortable bed with white linen sheets; she has a room of her own; she shares a bathroom with her employers and eats what they do, etc.; ibid.: 163). Similarly, Roy Armes points out that 'though she suffers *no real brutality*, she feels increasingly lonely and exploited' (2006: 69, my emphasis). Such comments, while perhaps technically correct, might miss the cleverness of Sembene's narrative and main character that unmask (pun intended) the insidiousness of the postcolonial era, which lacks the direct representation of colonial violence but remains equally brutal because it only gives the appearance of equality and progress. In short, there is nothing prosaic about this story.

It is the dual quality of the film, as both criticism of postcolonialism and forewarning about self-awareness, that would inspire generations of African film-makers. Narrative versions of Diouana abound in African cinemas and, aesthetically speaking, the motif of shadows is just one material example that visually reverberates in a slew of other films. To invoke but a few selective examples, Safi Faye's *Mossane* (1996) begins with a backlit shot of the main character who turns into a shadowy outline; Jean-Pierre Bekolo's *Les Saignantes* (2005) and Mati Diop's *Atlantique/Atlantics* (2019) present a wide array of women living in the shadows or as shadows themselves. In Alain Gomis's *Tey/Today* (2012), the main character, Satché, learns that he will die at the end of the day. Thierno Ndiaye Doss, who had portrayed the titular character in Sembene's *Guelwaar* (1992), plays the role of an 'uncle' who washes the dead, which is a part of the Muslim practices of mourning. When Satché visits him, they walk through the ritual together by mimicking the washing of the body. Just as Diouana begins to arrange her affairs prior to her suicide, Satché's mourning process predates the actual arrival of death.

*Black Girl* also continues to circulate around the world. Both the BFI and the Cinémathèque française in Paris screened the film as part of Sembene retrospectives commemorating one hundred years since the film-maker's birth in 1923.[50] From the perspective of legacy, the film's influence continues to grow, as evidenced by three recent African diasporic films, which also mark the shift towards the positive futures mentioned in the introduction and alluded to by the young politicians exiting the National Assembly in *Black Girl*.

The first example is Jordan Peele's glorious *Get Out* (2017).[51] The main character, Chris, is a photographer. Inside his apartment, where the film begins, there are several large-format photographs on the walls, presumably taken by him. The camera lingers on the image of a child wearing a mask, holding it to his face with two hands.

Get Out (2017)

As the camera slowly tracks back, the photograph gets smaller, and eventually Chris is revealed to the right of the frame, shaving in the bathroom. He, too, wears a quasi-mask of shaving cream. While there is no material proof that Peele thought about Sembene's *Black Girl*, the mask is an irrefutable trope in Black culture, harking back to W. E. B. Du Bois's concept of double consciousness.[52] Chris also plays two parts: as himself when he talks with his garrulous Black friend, and as someone who wears a mask when conversing with his girlfriend's white parents and friends. After the couple arrives at the mansion, the girlfriend's father shows Chris around, and there is a moment that echoes Monsieur's attitude towards other cultures: the father proudly holds two artifacts and exclaims that he picked them up in Bali. He then continues to explain that the decorations are 'eclectic' because he is a traveller. What Chris and the audience learn later is that among the items that the family likes to 'pick up' are actual Black people.

Second, in Maïmouna Doucouré's *Mignonnes/Cuties* (2020), the main character, Amy, aged only eleven, becomes enthralled with a group of pre-teen twerkers who hope to win a dance competition. Her mother is dealing with heartache, and, taking over the role of the missing father, an elderly 'aunt' gives very conservative advice. The aunt is played by Mbissine Thérèse Diop in a direct nod to Sembene and perhaps even to a version of Diouana who survived the pains of immigration but who turned callous and inflexible as a result. The beauty of the film lies in Amy's paradoxical odyssey, which echoes Diouana's: she lives in a world that seems open and full of possibilities (that is what the internet reminds her), but she is simultaneously bound by the religious traditions of older generations. Like Diouana before her, and despite being born in France, Amy is equally a prisoner and a victim.

The last example, and the one most unmistakably connected to the legacy of *Black Girl*, is Nikyatu Jusu's film *Nanny*. In it, Aisha, a Senegalese émigrée to the US, takes a job as a nanny with a white family, hoping to save enough to bring her young son to the country, too. There are several other links to *Black Girl*. First, the white employers, despite their suggestive name (Hav), never seem to have the money they owe Aisha. Second, Aisha has a vision of drowning in the bathtub – the place where Diouana takes her own life – and eventually she does try to kill herself by drowning. In another instance, Jusu films Aisha in the tub from an overhead, objective shot. Under water, the character is curled up in the foetal position, which conjures up simultaneous images of motherhood and infancy. Third, Adam Hav, the Monsieur of this film, makes an actual pass at Aisha, rendering real what only lurked beneath the surface in Sembene's film. Fourth, while sitting on a park bench Aisha overhears a couple of other nannies discussing the tragic case of a co-worker, Sonia. This woman apparently 'slit her employer's child's throat from ear to ear', which happens to be the exact expression used by Sembene in the short story ('with her throat cut from ear to ear'; 1987: 86).

Despite these similarities, Jusu's film stands on its own, as it deals in greater depth with another type of trauma, the loss of a child (the film's plot twist is its revelation that Aisha's son, Lamine, had drowned in the ocean). Nevertheless, it is worth noting that the film ends on a positive note, despite the harrowing disclosure and the fact that Aisha attempts to drown herself. Malik, her love interest, rescues her, and we find out in the denouement flash-forward that Aisha is pregnant. Moreover, Jusu expertly weaves into the narrative references to West African folklore and mythology by invoking the ambivalent figures of Mami Wata and Anansi the spider. The former especially – by virtue of her connection to water – appears several times in the film, haunting (or perhaps helping) Aisha.

The film's horror label is, on the one hand, in line with Jusu's earlier work (*Suicide by Sunlight* [2019] is a short vampire tale). On the other hand, it hints at the longevity of the colonial trauma – a horror that continues to plague the contemporary world. In other words, the intimacy shared between Diouana and the audience in 1966 no longer feels like a secret. Furthermore, the secret must no longer be relegated to the realm of voiceover, and Jusu involves the audience in a radically distinct manner: she looks to inflict Aisha's pain on all of us. The horror genre by and large speaks to our shared consciousness, our demons and traumas that take a variety of materialised forms (vampires, zombies, psychotic serial killers, etc.). In Sembene's film, Diouana's pain is to be understood, on one level, as primarily hers. On another level, the pain is to be extended figuratively to other Africans who had to navigate the complexities of the rapacious neoliberal order meant to perpetuate the dominance of the Global North. Jusu's film (like Peele's) sheds light on the current effects of these complexities and deals more directly with the pains and traumas of the Black race.

## Coda

During my visit to the Sembene archives at the Lilly Library on the Indiana University campus, I stumbled upon a letter from the BFI addressed to Ousmane Sembene and dated 1992. The then editor of the BFI Film Classics was inviting the director to write a book for this very series, on whatever film he wished. The archive contained no evidence of a reply, and so I have no idea if Sembene ever responded to the invitation, but obviously there is no BFI book penned by the Senegalese director. However, it is tempting to think that, had he done so, he would not have picked *Bicycle Thieves* or *The 400 Blows*. Instead, it would have been a film from the diasporic universe, which continues to expand thanks to directors like Peele, Doucouré and Jusu. If Sembene had had a chance to see their films, his prophetic words would have been validated, because the cinematic world does, even if only to a certain degree, still follow the light of Sembene-the-sun.

# Notes

**1** This comment is in stark contrast with the director's (earlier) preference for anonymity. Samba Gadjigo's biography sheds significant light on the notoriously closed-off Sembene, who is quoted as saying, 'The work I have done is what matters most. As to my poor self, I want to remain anonymous, lost among the crowd' (2010: xix).

**2** It would be difficult to summarise the film's reception, especially when it comes to the more recent reviews and reactions, as it is probably the most written-about African visual text. In 1966, the journal *Le Monde* praised the film for winning the Jean Vigo prize. However, in the US, critic Roger Ebert widely panned the film, calling it a 'slow and pedestrian affair', and quipping that the director may have 'learned filmmaking by making this film' (1969). In the academic world, Marie-Claire Wuilleumier wrote that the film offered an 'original dimension' compared to other African films (1967: 137). In the contemporary period, though, Sembene's film has reached critical consensus – this is one of the most consequential films in the history of cinema. Moreover, various flagship newspapers, such as the *New York Times* or the *Guardian*, generally commend the 'vision' and 'ingenuity' of the director (Scott 2016), or the 'expressive tone' of the film (Hoffman 2016).

**3** See also David Murphy's separate notes about the name (2001: 1).

**4** Gadjigo notes that Sembene's birthplace 'holds a prominent place in his imagination' (2010: 5) and reminds us that Diouana comes from the same region. Historically, Casamance is a place known for its 'rebellious attitude toward any central authority' (ibid.: 10), and to Gadjigo, Sembene's naming of his own house *Gallè Ceddo* (the house of the rebel) points to the 'spirit of revolt' and 'desire for freedom' (ibid.) that define the artist's lifework.

**5** For a complete study of the *tirailleur* motif, see David Murphy's essay 'Fighting for the Homeland?' In it, Murphy specifies that Sembene 'saw action in Europe in the final years of the Second World War' (2007: 67n3).However, according to Gadjigo, Sembene's *tirailleur* assignment at 'the Artillery Annex in Niamey' only involved 'transportation of troops […] notably in Morrocco – by way of Algeria' (2010: 61).

**6** More than enough has already been written about Sembene's Marxism, so I will limit myself to very few additional comments. At the Indiana University Sembene archives, I found an image of Sembene wearing a Che Guevara T-shirt. The same image appears as a poster on the set of *Xala*, but does not make the final cut (see p. 12). However, the character played by Sembene – a translator and notary – in *Mandabi* has a large photo of young Guevara covering his desk. According to Gadjigo's interview for Criterion, Marxism gave the director a grander purpose (and, it must be said, with less violent connotations in comparison with Che): to tackle contemporary issues meant to support the complete liberation of Africa by way of film. As Murphy and Williams note, 'Sembene's Marxism must also be seen within the context of his profound pan-Africanism, a belief in the unity of purpose and destiny of the different peoples of his continent' (2007: 55). Finally, in the original screenplay for the film, Sembene appears to have scribbled a quote attributed to Marx on the back of the last page: 'The writer, the artist must naturally make money to live and write, but he must not under any circumstance live and write to make money' (see p. 13).

**7** In the post-independence period, the French National Centre of Cinema (CNC) – a cultural agency responsible for the production and promotion of cinema in France – offered modest financial backing to films from the French colonies. 'Domirev' was Sembene's own film company, most often spelled as *Films Domireew. Les Actualités Françaises* was a French TV company based in Paris. For more on the history of the CNC, see Roy Armes (2006: 53–60) and Daniela Ricci (2020: 45–8).

**8** One should perhaps not take Sembene's declaration as an absolute. While it is true that the most circulated version of the film is completely in black and white, other versions remain in existence and they include one colour sequence (for example, the copies at the Museum of Modern Art in New York and the BFI).

**9** The Walker Art Museum in Minneapolis held a Sembene retrospective in 2011, hosted by Charles Sugnet. In introducing *Black Girl*, Sugnet shared that the film was shot in only twenty days, and it cost the equivalent

of twenty thousand dollars. The CFA (Communauté Financière Africaine) was introduced to the French colonies in the 1940s. By the 1960s the CFA franc had depreciated tremendously, as evident from the discrepancy between the sum mentioned by Sembene and the number cited by Sugnet.

**10** Sembene had to produce *Mandabi* in French as a condition of its financing, but he simultaneously shot a version in Wolof, which remains in wide circulation to this day.

**11** Sembene is responsible for an important decolonial project – the creation of the first newspaper in Wolof (*Kaddu*, meaning 'Word'), which is visible on p. 12.

**12** My translation of '*Le film africain, né en 1924, renaît entre 1953 et 1957 et commence à se développer après l'indépendance des pays africains.*'

**13** The vast majority were from Dakar (see the charts beginning on p. 400; Vieyra 1975).

**14** For Gabriel, they were called 'unqualified assimilation' (as in, copying Hollywood), 'the remembrance phase' (a more bellicose attitude that aimed to reject the 'ways of the past') and the 'combative phase' (1989: 31–5). Diawara went with 'social realism', 'colonial confrontation' and 'return to the source' (1992: 160). The three categories, while reductive, helped the public understand how the concept of Third Cinema took shape at the intersection of several key themes of postcolonial theory: memory, identity, history and hybridity.

**15** Loosely defined, Third Cinema performs resistance both thematically (by criticising colonialism, its after-effects and by rewriting history from an indigenous perspective) and stylistically (by responding to mainstream cinema and to auteur cinema). For more on this, see the manifesto *Towards a Third Cinema* (1969), by Fernando Getino and Octavio Solanas.

**16** '*Le temps de l'Afrique viendra*' (Africa's turn will come; Mbembe 2013: 252).

**17** Sembene belatedly shifts towards the sonic, having already established Diouana as a purely visual object upon her arrival. Nevertheless, once the audience is introduced to Diouana's voice, we experience the story as sound first, image second, in contrast with the traditional way in which we register cinematic meaning (i.e. image comes first, then sound is simply an add-on meant to complete or support the meaning of the visual). For more on the history of sound cinema, see the introduction to my book *Sonic Space* (2017), pp. 1–41.

**18** In an interview with Ukadike, Mambety explains that 'Cinema was born in Africa, because the image itself was born in Africa. The instruments, yes, are European, but the creative necessity and rationale exist in our oral tradition' (2002: 128–9). For more on African orality, see Ukadike (1994: 203).

**19** Tobias Warner also explains that the limited budget prevented Ms Diop from travelling to Paris to record the dialogue (2017: 115), which matches Gadjigo's account.

**20** My translation of '*Voix de désir, de doute et de chair.*'

**21** In *City Lights* (1931), Chaplin's Tramp swallows a whistle, which Slavoj Žižek reads as being an uncontrollable excess of the body. Sound coming out of someone can thus be completely autonomous and, moreover, it can make the brain register shame. The reference to Chaplin is not haphazard, as I will return to other connections with Sembene shortly.

**22** This does not appear to be the case with the two white actors playing Madame and Monsieur, as Tobias Warner notes (2017: 116). Warner also calls Diouana's voice 'almost extra-diegetic' (for more about the 'disconnect' between body and voice, see pages 115–17).

**23** The fact that Sembene foregrounds Diouana's voice strongly evokes the oral tradition of African tales. Like Sembene, Diouana is a storyteller, the *griotte* of her own life.

**24** *Borom Sarret* follows the life of a cart driver over the course of a day. The quasi-odyssey eventually takes him to the 'Plateau', where he is not allowed to go and where a cop confiscates the cart.

**25** Sembene recycles the tune for the soundtrack of *Mandabi*. It may be worth noting that the soundtrack for *Black Girl* includes a song in Serer, a Senegambian dialect common in the south of Senegal.

**26** '*Jamais plus de Diouana*' translates more accurately to 'no more Diouana', which more clearly announces the intent to commit suicide.

**27** The poem is written in free verse, which textually matches its content and references to 'liberty' and to the 'proud African girl'. Sembene also emphasises the presence of the community by repeatedly highlighting the possessive pronoun 'our' (1987: 99–101).

**28** Warner explains that Gomis is a 'Manjak surname […] originally from plurilingual Casamance' (2017: 117–18).

**29** Murphy and Williams describe Sembene's first films as 'literary', because they resort to a narrative voiceover (2007: 51).

**30** In fairness, Diouana judges everyone at the dinner party when she thinks to herself that 'all they do is drink'.

**31** There are other instances when Diouana expresses annoyance. When they first begin to interact, she notes that he would not stop talking. When she follows this remark with 'I promised I would see him again,' it might be less evidence of genuine interest and more of a way to shut him up. The same logic later applies to her decision to sleep with him.

**32** The version I use as reference is the one held at the Sembene archives (Lilly Library, Indiana University).

**33** My translation of '*Pourquoi boude-t-il? Je suis chez lui. Que veut-il de plus? Je dois aller en France. J'ai promis à ma patronne!*'

**34** The poem at the end of the short story invokes the ancestors directly (Sembene 1987: 101), placing Diouana in the transitional realm. Murphy and Williams also note that the 'mask worn by the young boy who follows him' is 'ghostly' (2007: 52).

**35** Others have invalidated, and more eloquently, the use of the pernicious term 'authentic' in relation to African film-making (see Tcheuyap 2011a; Harrow 2007, 2015).

**36** Sembene changed these details from the short story, which describes Monsieur's living room as a 'hunter's den' (Sembene 1987: 84). Cultural appropriation replaces the more violent implications of trophy hunting.

**37** Most associated with Alfred Hitchcock, who popularised it, the MacGuffin is a plot device. Slavoj Žižek calls it 'nothing at all', 'an empty place' and 'a pure pretext for setting the action in motion' (1989: 163, 182).

**38** My translation of '*Le suicide* […] *n'a pu avoir lieu que parce que l'individu se trouve hors de la communauté vivante.*'

**39** Mati Diop's *Mille soleils/A Thousand Suns* (2013) imagines a fictional world in which Anta lives in Canada, but there is no indication about her overall life satisfaction.

**40** This accusation represents a reversal from the short story, in which it is Madame who calls the maid a liar (Sembene 1987: 99). The personal attack is the last straw for Diouana.

**41** Like Sembene, Diouana is probably Muslim. While Sembene was raised as a Muslim, he self-identified as an atheist later in life.

**42** The future is missing from this equation. Diouana's wish to have her photograph taken by the beach to send back home never materialises, and thus she is denied the (photographed) future version of herself.

**43** The main quintet of French New Wave auteurs – Truffaut, Godard, Chabrol, Rohmer and Rivette – often resorted to intertextual references to each other's work.

**44** Chaplin is conspicuous as an outlier in the series of historically significant African leaders. The inclusion likely has to do with Chaplin's well-documented cinematic influence on several francophone directors, Mambety and Mahamat-Saleh Haroun to mention but two. In Diawara's documentary, Sembene, too, discusses his appreciation of Chaplin's prodigious knowledge of film history.

**45** Orson Welles's *Citizen Kane* (1941) and Akira Kurosawa's *Rashomon* had already made great use of triangles to give structure and meaning to shot composition. The latter features an eerily similar shot, through the legs of the 'bandit', with the two other main characters visible in the background.

**46** The same applies to Madame. In the first flashback, Diouana recounts meeting her, while waiting in the street alongside other women. When Madame shows up, she evaluates the group from behind sunglasses, making our heroine remark in voiceover, 'No one could see her eyes.'

**47** For a more detailed reading of the moment, see Williams's excellent analysis (2024: 72–5).

**48** Rama attends Cheikh Anta Diop University, denounces imported items from France and responds in Wolof to her father's diatribes in French. Faat invests her time, energy and money in a local business, having raised a son, Djib, who dreams of becoming the next president of the republic.

**49** My translation of '*cache la profondeur de la réflexion de l'auteur sur la condition sociale en Afrique et le drame auquel l'Afrique a à faire face*'.

**50** Similar events took place across North America: the Toronto Film Festival Cinematheque, the Harvard Film Archive, the Berkeley Art Museum and the Pacific Film Archive, to name but a few, programmed retrospectives of Sembene's films in late 2023/early 2024. It may also be worth mentioning that in 2009 the magazine *Africultures* ran a lengthy tribute, titled *Sembène Ousmane (1923–2007)*. The dossier, which featured interventions by Boubacar Boris Diop, Olivier Barlet, David Murphy, Sada Niang and several others, helped cement the director's legacy as one of the most consequential artists of our time.

**51** Coincidentally, these two films, Sembene's and Peele's, featured in a tie at number ninety-five in the 2022 *Sight and Sound* Greatest Films of All Time poll.

**52** The mask trope makes a return in Peele's *Us* (2019), in which a young boy, Jason, wears a wolf-like mask throughout the film. For an example from literature, see Ben Okri's short story, 'A Wrinkle in the Realm' (2021), about a Black man who decides to wear masks to deal with social anxieties and other people's misperceptions of him.

# Credits

**La Noire de .../**
**Black Girl**
Senegal/France
1966

**Director**
Ousmane Sembene
**Producer**
André Zwobada
**Assistant Director**
Ibrahima Barro
Pathé Diop
**Script**
Ousmane Sembene
based on a novella by
Ousmane Sembene
**Director of Photography**
Christian Lacoste
**Editor**
André Gaudier
**Production Company**
Filmi Domirev
Les Actualités Françaises
**Production Manager**
André Zwobada

**CAST**
**Mbissine Thérèse Diop**
Diouana
**Anne-Marie Jelinek**
Madame
**Robert Fontaine**
Monsieur
**Momar Nar Sene**
the young man
**Ibrahima Boy**
boy with mask
**Bernard Delbard**
**Nicole Donati**
**Raymond Lemeri**
**Suzanne Lemeri**
guests
**Philippe**
**Sophie**
**Damien**
children
**Toto Bissainthe**
voiceover
dubbed voice of Diouana
**Robert Marcy**
dubbed voice of
Monsieur
**Sophie Leclair**
dubbed voice of Madame

*uncredited*
**Ousmane Sembene**
the teacher

**Production Details**
35mm
1.37:1
Black and white/Colour
Mono
Running time:
59 minutes

**Release Details**
Senegal theatrical
release on 17 March 1966
France theatrical release
on 5 April 1967

# Bibliography

Armes, Roy (2006), *African Filmmaking: North and South of the Sahara* (Bloomington: Indiana University Press).

Barlet, Olivier (1996), *Les Cinémas d'Afrique noire: le regard en question* (Paris: Images Plurielles).

Barlet, Olivier and Claude Forest (2023), 'Key Dates in the History of African Cinema', in Michael T. Martin and Gaston Kaboré (eds), *African Cinema: Manifesto and Practice for Cultural Decolonization. Volume 1: Colonial Antecedents, Constituents, Theory, and Articulations* (Bloomington: Indiana University Press), pp. 419–60.

Bazin, André (1971), *What Is Cinema?*, trans. Hugh Gray (Berkeley: University of California Press).

Calhoun, Doyle (2021), 'Sembène's "Black Girl" Is a Ghost Story', *Public Books* (4 November). Available at: <https://www.publicbooks.org/sembenes-black-girl-is-a-ghost-story/> (accessed 20 March 2023).

Chion, Michel (1999), *The Voice in Cinema* (New York: Columbia University Press).

Diawara, Manthia (1992), *African Cinema: Politics & Culture* (Bloomington: Indiana University Press).

Dima, Vlad (2017), *Sonic Space in Djibril Diop Mambety's Films* (Bloomington: Indiana University Press).

Dolar, Mladen (2006), *A Voice and Nothing More* (Boston: Massachusetts Institute of Technology Press).

Ebert, Roger (1969), '*Black Girl/Borom Sarret* movie review', RogerEbert.com (9 October). Available at: <https://www.rogerebert.com/reviews/black-girl--borom-sarret-1969> (accessed 25 July 2024).

Gabriel, Teshome (1989), 'Towards a Critical Theory of Third World Films', in Jim Pines and Paul Willemen (eds), *Questions of Third Cinema* (London: BFI), pp. 30–52.

Gadjigo, Samba (2010), *Ousmane Sembène: The Making of a Militant Artist*, trans. Moustapha Diop (Bloomington: Indiana University Press).

Gamalinda, Sarah (2022), *Race Shapes: Racial In/Visibility in Contemporary Francophone Literature and Cinema* (PhD dissertation/ProQuest) (Madison: University of Wisconsin).

Genova, James (2013), *Cinema and Development in West Africa* (Bloomington: Indiana University Press).

Harrow, Kenneth (2007), *Postcolonial African Cinema: From Political Engagement to Postmodernism* (Bloomington: Indiana University Press).

—— (2015), 'Manthia Diawara's Waves and the Problem of the "Authentic"', *African Studies Review* 58, no. 3, pp. 13–30.

Hennebelle, Guy (2008), 'Ousmane Sembène: For Me, the Cinema Is an Instrument of Political Action, but…', in Annett Busch and Max Annas (eds), *Ousmane Sembène: Interviews* (Jackson: University Press of Mississippi), pp. 7–17.

Hoffman, Jordan (2016), '*Black Girl* review – Ousmane Sembène's film dazzles 50 years on', *Guardian*, 18 May. Available at: <https://

www.theguardian.com/film/2016/
may/18/black-girl-review-ousmene-
sembene-groundbreaking?>
(accessed 25 July 2024).

Mbembe, Achille (2013), *Sortir de
la grande nuit: essai sur l'Afrique
décolonisée* (Paris: Éditions de la
découverte/Poche).

—— (2023), 'Circulations', in Achille
Mbembe and Felwine Sarr (eds),
*The Politics of Time: Imagining African
Becomings*, trans. Philip Gerard
(Cambridge: Polity Press), pp. 85–95.

Murphy, David (2001), *Sembene: Imagining
Alternatives in Film & Fiction* (Trenton,
NJ: Africa World Press).

—— (2007), 'Fighting for the Homeland?
The Second World War in the Films
of Ousmane Sembene', *L'Esprit
Créateur* 47, no. 1, pp. 56–67.

Murphy, David and Patrick Williams
(2007), *Postcolonial African Cinema:
Ten Directors* (Manchester:
Manchester University Press).

Pfaff, Françoise (1996), 'Eroticism and
Sub-Saharan African Films', in
Imruh Bakari and Mbye B. Cham
(eds), *African Experiences of Cinema*
(London: BFI), pp. 252–61.

—— (2004), 'African Cities as Cinematic
Texts', in Françoise Pfaff (ed.),
*Focus on African Films* (Bloomington:
Indiana University Press),
pp. 89–106.

Ricci, Daniela (2020), *African Diasporic
Cinema: Aesthetics of Reconstruction*,
trans. Melissa Thackway (East
Lansing: Michigan State University
Press).

Sarr, Felwine (2016), *Afrotopia* (Paris:
Éditions Philippe Rey).

—— (2023), 'Reopening Futures', in
Achille Mbembe and Felwine Sarr
(eds), *The Politics of Time: Imagining
African Becomings*, trans. Philip Gerard
(Cambridge: Polity Press), pp. 117–28.

Scott, A.O. (2016), 'Ousmane Sembène's
*Black Girl* turns 50', *New York Times*,
17 May. Available at: <https://www.
nytimes.com/2016/05/18/movies/
ousmane-sembenes-black-girl-
turns-50.html> (accessed 25 July
2024).

Sembene, Ousmane (1987), 'The
Promised Land', in *Tribal Scars and
Other Stories*, trans. Len Ortzen
(Portsmouth, NH: Heinemann),
pp. 84–101.

Smith, Clint (2021), *How the Word Is
Passed: A Reckoning with the History
of Slavery Across America* (New York:
Little, Brown and Company).

Tcheuyap, Alexie (2011a), *Postnationalist
African Cinemas* (Manchester:
Manchester University Press).

—— (2011b), 'African Cinema(s)', *Critical
Interventions* 5, no. 1, pp. 10–26.

Thackway, Melissa (2003), *Africa Shoots
Back: Alternative Perspectives in Sub-
Saharan Francophone African Film*
(Bloomington: Indiana University
Press).

Ukadike, N. Frank (1994), *Black African
Cinema* (Berkeley: University of
California Press).

—— (2002), *Questioning African Cinema:
Conversations with Filmmakers*
(Minneapolis: University of
Minnesota Press).

Vieyra, Paulin Soumanou (1969),
*Le Cinéma et l'Afrique* (Paris: Présence
Africaine).

—— (1975), *Le Cinéma africain: des origines à 1973* (Paris: Présence Africaine).

—— (2012), *Sembène Ousmane, cinéaste. Première période, 1962–1971* (Paris: Présence Africaine).

Warner, Tobias (2017), 'Enacting Postcolonial Translation: Voice, Color and Free Indirect Discourse in the Restored Version of Ousmane Sembene's *La Noire de …*', in Judith Misrahi-Barak and Srilata Ravi (eds), *Translating the Postcolonial in Multilingual Contexts* (Montpellier: Presses universitaires de la Méditerranée), pp. 113–26.

Williams, James S. (2024), *Xala* (London: BFI/Bloomsbury).

Wuilleumier, Marie-Claire (1967), 'Naissance d'un cinéma', *Esprit* 362, no. 7–8 (July–August), pp. 135–40.

Žižek, Slavoj (1989), *The Sublime Object of Ideology* (London: Verso).

—— (1996), '"I Hear You with My Eyes"; or, The Invincible Master', in Renata Salecl and Slavoj Žižek (eds), *Gaze and Voice as Love Objects* (Durham, NC: Duke University Press), pp. 90–127.